London's
Parks & Gardens

by Nana Ocran

London's Parks and Gardens

Written by Nana Ocran
Photography by Natalie Pecht
Cover photographs by Ryan Wood
(other photo credits see p. 192)
Edited by Abigail Willis
Design by Susi Koch & Lesley Gilmour
Maps by Lesley Gilmour
Cover Design by The Partners

Published 2006 by

 Metro Publications
PO Box 6336
London
N1 6PY

Printed and bound in India
© Metro Publication 2006

British Library Cataloguing in Publication Data.
A catalogue record for this book is available from the British Library.

ISBN   1 902910 19 2

dedicated to my family

Acknowledgements

Thanks are due to the following people who I feel were a huge help during the research and writing of this book. Ndidi for listening through the different stages of my research and writing, Gaylene for sharing my enthusiasm and my Dad for giving me early inspiration to write.

Numerous organisations have helped me research this book. My thanks go to London Metropolitan Archives, City of Westminster Archives Centre, Corporation of London (Susan Banks), Wandsworth Borough Council, Lambeth Borough Council, Hammersmith and Fulham Council, Haringey Council, Greater London Authority, BBC London, London Development Agency, Visit London, Peckham Rye Park Environment and Leisure Department (Eleonora Oliva).

Metro Publications would like to thank Trish, Jack, Bob and all those at The Partners that have contributed to the design of our new covers and logo.

Map Key

	Footpath		War Memorial
	Main path/road		Viewpoint
	Bridal path	**P**	Parking
	Cycle path		Toilets
	Athletics track		Refreshments
	Swimming		Children's playground
	Fountain		Sport's pitches
	Bandstand		Tennis courts

Contents

Introduction

Strangely enough, I've pretty much always thought of a park as just a park. A convenient green space to chill out in the absence of a garden, or to escape from the confines of an office, which has always meant latching on to whichever park is most local to where I live or work.

However, in writing this book, I wanted to provide something of a balance between the four corners of London. This has meant viewing the capital in a more expansive way, unearthing London's character through some of the stories that have been generated by centuries of use of its outdoor spaces.

It's not just buildings that give London its character. The city's open spaces are a world within a world with the various strands of park life being particularly active during the summer months, when cyclists, runners, picnickers, sunbathers et al pack out the avenues, woodlands, lawns and meadows. Often the bigger the park, or the better the facilities the larger the crowds, but with each individual green space, there often comes a particular type of visitor. It was lovely to see people practicing yoga or Tai Chi by the Buddhist Peace Pagoda in Battersea Park, seasoned kite flyers on Hampstead Heath, lunchtime office workers scrutinising the hand-lettered tiles in Postman's Park, or earnest walkers heading into or out of Queens Wood, Epping Forest or the woodland areas of Osterley Park. Sports grounds, boating lakes and even paddling pools – the ones that actually open during the usually brief summer – help generate a fleeting al fresco culture. Dusk is a particularly good time for strolling, especially in the smaller parks where you have fewer worries about reaching the exits before being locked in for the night.

But then again, it's not all about the spring and summer months or the sunshine. Autumn and winter bring a completely new vibe to the parks, which although more sparsely populated in cold weather, are still oases of contemplation. A September visit to Green Park meant stepping through blankets of auburn leaves on the extensive tree-dotted lawns, while pre-Christmas frost on the dramatic hills of Alexandra Palace Park in the north was mirrored by the crisp white hilly mounds of Greenwich Park down south.

With such a broad spectrum of park locations and sizes, it was a pleasure but also a challenge to negotiate the multiple acres. The task was not made any easier by the often minimal presence of park keepers or outdoor staff who might have been able to expand on the key characteristics of their territory. However, a few local and specialist archives (see page 192) were excellent resources for unearthing 326 years of facts and fictions of London's parks, gardens and squares, which are provided in the 'Did you Know' boxes. From royal hunts, executions and demonstrations to festivals and film shoots, these spaces turned out to have plenty of stories to tell.

Whatever the season or size of the park some things were constant. Sadly in many of the larger or medium sized places, the familiar bandstands – a feature of many open green spaces – were clearly unused. These faded theatrical landmarks were often fenced or scaffolded off, or stood alone like out of use toys.

Aside from the picturesque and calming tree lined avenues, lush bushes and borders to be found in many parks, it was the unique character of some of the parks that stood out. Childhood memories of searching the ruins of Crystal Palace were rekindled by walking the length of the preserved terraces that once framed the massive Victorian glasshouse. The first-time visits to west London's beautifully laid out Emslie Horniman Pleasance and the community-created Meanwhile Gardens on the edge of a section of the Grand Union Canal, remain in the memory. I was also won over by east London's Springfield Park with its excellent family-run café and canal links to Lee Valley. Streatham Rookery, tucked away inside the SW16 common, is like a secret garden; while the quirky designs of Phoenix Garden, a communal patch of green behind the bustle of Charing Cross Road, was another great find. I hope with the aid of this book you can discover and treasure a few of London's wonderful parks and gardens.

St James's Park

London's Parks

Hyde Park

London's Parks Map

FINSBURY

FINSBURY
PARK

STOKE
NEWINGTON

SPRINGFIELD
PARK

LEYTONHAM

CLISSOLD
PARK

ABNEY
PARK

CAMLEY STREET
NATURAL PARK

ISLINGTON

HACKNEY
VICTORIA
PARK

WEST HA
WEST HAM
PARK

HAGGERSTON
PARK

CORAM'S
FIELDS

POSTMAN'S
PARK

SHOREDITCH

STEPNEY

MILE END
PARK

PHOENIX
GARDENS

EEN
RK

MES'S
ARK

TIBETAN
PEACE GARDEN

DEPTFORD

GREENWICH
ECOLOGY PARK

LAMBETH

BURGESS
PARK

GREENWICH

GREENWICH
PARK

VAUXHALL
PARK

MYATTS'S
FIELDS

CAMBERWELL

PECKHAM RYE
COMMON

LEWISHAM

APHAM

RUSKIN
PARK

WINDMILL
GARDENS

SUNRAY
GARDENS

PECKHAM RYE
PARK

DULWICH

SUNRAY
GARDENS

BROCKWELL
PARK

DULWICH
PARK

HORNIMAN
GARDENS

CATFORD

BEC
N

WEST
NORWOOD

SYDENHAM
WELL GARDENS

STREATHAM
COMMON

STREATHAM
ROOKERY

CRYSTAL
PALACE

CRYSTAL PALACE
PARK

Central London

St James's Park

Coram's Fields

Area: Approx 7 acres
93 Guilford Street, WC1
Tel: 020 7837 6138
Transport: Russell Square LU
Open: Daily 9am-8pm (May-Aug) and 9am-4.30pm (Sept-April)
Facilities: Football pitch, basketball courts, farm, paddling pool,
playground
Café

London's famous children's park in WC1 caters to all those up to eighteen years – with signs warning lone adults against entry. Formerly a Foundling Hospital for abandoned children, the site was the brainchild of philanthropist Thomas Coram, who set up the orphanage in 1747. Demolished in 1920, it wasn't until 1936 that this became a children's play area.

Enclosed by a high white wall and an L-shaped terraced building (used for occasional Corporate functions), it's well obscured by the road, so that the internal seven acres, which include a paddling pool, playground, climbing equipment and café can all be enjoyed in safety. Astro Turf for football games and a basketball court are popular with the older children.

There's also a farm, with bantam chickens, goats, ducks, geese and guinea pigs, as well as sheep brought over from Spitalfields City Farm, who like to graze on the grass beyond their enclosure. Signs warn children to contain their energy when it comes to the park's fountain, which endured its fair share of repair work due to persistent standing on the source of the water jets. Along with lone adults, dogs are also denied access to the park, and thanks to these precautions, this is a lively, safe and thriving area throughout the year where children can take advantage of the play equipment, turn their hands to gardening in an ongoing wildlife project, or enjoy visiting bands and circus acts in the summer.

Green Park

Area: Approx 40 acres
Between Constitution Hill and Piccadilly, SW1
Tel: 020 7930 1793
Transport: Green Park LU, Hyde Park Corner LU; Bus 2, 8, 9, 14, 16,
19, 22, 38, 52, 73, 82
Open: Daily 24 hours
Mobile Café

Not quite as fabulous as the adjacent St James's Park with its lake, swans and flowerbeds, Green Park has nonetheless come a long way since its days as a 16th-century plague pit. The place was known for its duels and highwaymen in the 18th century, but nowadays nature supplies the wow factor. Blankets of daffodils carpet the park in spring and drifts of copper coloured leaves cover the lawns in autumn, which look especially beautiful on the slopes that lead downward towards Victoria. Surrounded by Piccadilly and Constitution Hill, Green Park is separated from the larger St James's Park by the Mall, and although it has a general absence of fancy flowerbeds, it's a peaceful haven for walks as well as being popular with joggers for its many paths lined with London planes, limes and silver maples. It's also a good central London link to the far larger Hyde Park. Formerly known as Upper St James's Park, Green Park once had families of deer, a ranger's house, ice house and two temples, both of which burnt down in the 18th and 19th centuries. There's nothing in the way of landmark buildings left, but the park does have the Canada memorial site at its Constitution Hill entrance. From a distance it looks like a mini silver ski-slope set into the lawns beside the large Canada Gates in front of Buckingham Palace. The memorial actually consists of two triangular slabs of polished black stone with shallow cascades of water and stencilled maple leaves. In front of the palace itself, there's also the awesome gold-topped monument to Queen Victoria, which can be spotted from as far back as the park's north entrance by the Ritz Hotel, near Green Park tube.

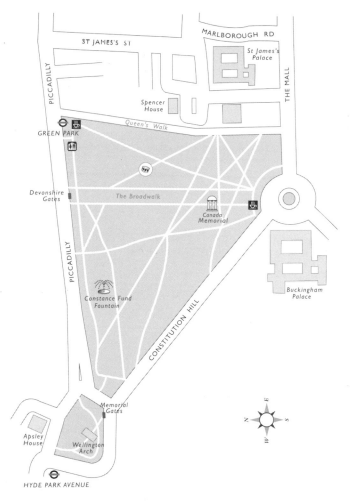

Hyde Park and Kensington Gardens

Kensington Gardens

Area: Approx 275 acres
Between Bayswater Road and Kensington Gore, W8
Tel: 020 7298 2100
Transport: Bayswater, High Street Kensington, Lancaster Gate or
Queensway LU; Bus 9, 12, 28, 49, 148
Open: Daily 6am-midnight
Facilities: Diana Memorial Playground
Café

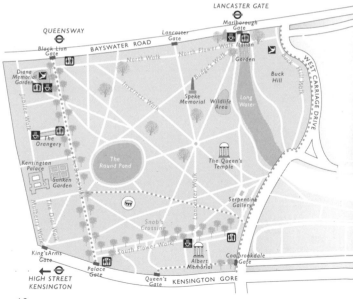

Hyde Park

Area: Approx 630 acres
Hyde Park, W2
Tel: 020 7298 2100 or 020 7262 3474 (sports facilities)
Transport: Hyde Park Corner, Knightsbridge, Lancaster Gate or
Marble Arch LU; Bus 2, 8, 10, 12, 23, 38, 73, 94
Open: Daily 5am to midnight
Facilities: Lido and paddling pool, 6 tennis courts in the sports centre,
bowling green, putting green, horse riding track, boating lake
Café/restaurant

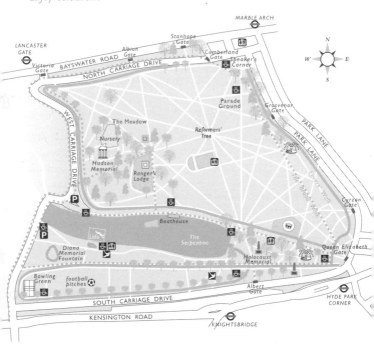

13

Hyde Park's sprawling 630 acre green space incorporates Kensington Gardens as well as being home to a beguiling mix of lawns, gardens, sculpture and horse tracks. This Royal Park is also a venue for some of London's most distinctive annual events such as the BBC Family Prom in the Park, charity runs like the Cancer Research UK Stride for Life and live gigs by bands, which have included R.E.M. A popular site for protest marches, it is also the home of Speakers' Corner, at the Marble Arch end of the park. On Sundays since the mid 19th century agitated speakers and often equally animated hecklers have exercised their right to speak publicly concerning anything that takes their fancy.

Once an exclusive hunting ground for Henry VIII, the park was at one time an area preserved specifically for the well-heeled. The Serpentine lake runs between Hyde Park and Kensington Gardens and is straddled by a bridge that divides the lake's southern end from the narrower Long Water section, beyond which lie the extravagant Italian Gardens. This ornate terrace has carved water nymphs, Neptune-like bearded males, four pools, spurting fountains, benches and overlooking the scene, a statue of Edward Jenner by William Calder Marshall. A renowned doctor in his lifetime, Jenner discovered the vaccine for smallpox in 1806. His statue, which had a brief stay in Trafalgar Square (1858–1862), was the first to be erected in Kensington Gardens in 1862. Down at the lake's southern end is Rotten Row, a four mile sandy track for horse riders who can book in for lessons at the Hyde Park Stables (020 7723 2813) or at Ross Nye's Riding Stables (020 7262 3791), both near Lancaster Gate tube.

The Serpentine is popular for boating and sailing and also has its fair share of wildfowl. The Serpentine Swimming Club *(www.serpentineswimmingclub.com)*, has been going since 1864, also puts this lake on the map. Swimmers can roll up to the water's edge at 8am every Saturday, even during the worst winters when the layers of ice get enthusiastically broken by some of the most determined dippers. One long-running tradition is the 100-yard race, which is

Kensington Palace

held every Christmas morning, with the winner picking up the Peter Pan cup – which used to be presented by the character's creator JM Barrie. If you're after a more serene swimming experience, the Serpentine Lido is a 60 metre pool that opens from June to September for swimming and children's paddling. Conveniently attached to a busy restaurant and café, it's also within easy reach of the Princess Diana Memorial Fountain, complete with its troubling health and safety issues. Towards Bayswater is the Princess Diana Memorial Playground (020 7298 2117), a sanctuary for youngsters, with adults allowed only rationed access to the area's pirate ship, water fountain and tree house from 9.30am to 10am daily.

Popular landmarks within the Hyde Park and Kensington Gardens include the Albert Memorial with its 180 feet, gold-encrusted spire, the Serpentine Gallery for contemporary art and family workshops and the bronze Peter Pan statue at the edge of the

Long Water. Further allegiance to Princess Diana's memory comes with the seven-mile Memorial Walk, which meanders through Kensington Gardens, Hyde Park, St James's Park and Green Park. Seventy plaques mark a number of locations that were important in the Princess's life, including Kensington Palace, where the offices and private apartments of members of the Royal Family are found, Clarence House which is Prince Charles's official London home and the private mansion of Spencer House in the heart of St James's.

Did you know?

During the 17th century, Oliver Cromwell regularly rode in Hyde Park, and was almost killed when he fell from his carriage and was dragged along behind it. Even worse, a loaded pistol went off in his pocket. In 1724 200,000 people flocked to Hyde Park to see the highwayman Jack Sheppard hung from the Tyburn Tree, which was also known as the Tyburn Gallows.

In 1816, Harriet Westbrook, the pregnant wife of poet Percy Bysshe Shelley, drowned herself in the Serpentine in Kensington Gardens, after learning that her husband had eloped with his 16-year-old mistress Mary Godwin. Mary went on to become Mrs Shelley and the author of the novel Frankenstein.

The Albert Memorial in Kensington Gardens was constructed in 1861 as a national memorial to Queen Victoria's husband, the Prince Regent. The book in his hand represents the catalogue of the 1851 Great Exhibition that took place in Hyde Park.

In the 1820s, a man with a shirt marked with 'S.T. Coleridge' was found hanging from a tree in Hyde Park. The papers reported that the poet Samuel Taylor Coleridge had died, much to the poet's surprise, who heard two men discussing his death in a coffee house. It turned out that the shirt did belong to Coleridge, who'd lost it a few years before.

Two Assassination attempts were made on Queen Victoria in the early 1840s as she drove through Hyde Park. Firstly, by would-be assassin barman Edward Oxford, who was sent to an asylum, and secondly by John Francis, who was transported for life.

In the summer of 1854, crowds regularly gathered at Hyde Park to protest against the Sunday Trading Bill, which was designed to end shopping on Sundays. It was dropped in 1855.

In the 1860s, Catherine Walters was one of the best known society prostitutes. She made her name by posing in Hyde Park for a Mayfair livery stable to advertise its horses. She wore a 'skin tight outfit with no underwear'.

Photographer Robert Freeman did a photo shoot with The Beatles in Hyde Park in 1964. Two of the images were used on the cover of the Beatles *For Sale* album, which was released in December of that year.

On 29 June 1968, Pink Floyd gave London's largest free concert in Hyde Park to promote their new album *A Saucerful of Secrets*.

On 5 July 1969 The Rolling Stones played a free concert for over 250,000 people by the Serpentine in Hyde Park. Three days before, their sacked guitarist Brian Jones had died.

On 14 Dec 1969, John Lennon and Yoko Ono turned up at Speakers' Corner in Hyde Park in a white Rolls-Royce. Both of them huddled inside a sealed white bag with a label 'A Silent Protest for James Hanratty' (who was convicted of murder) attached to it.

In July 1980, a massive IRA explosion killed a mounted group of the Household Cavalry as they rode through Hyde Park. Two hours later, six bandsmen of the Royal Green Jackets were blown up as they played in Regent's Park

In 2003, over one million people marched to Hyde Park to demonstrate against the war in Iraq.

Phoenix Gardens

Phoenix Gardens

Area: Approx 0.5 acres
21 Stacey Street, WC2
Tel: 020 7379 3187
Transport: Tottenham Court Road LU
Open: Daily dawn til dusk

This peaceful community garden snuggling within the surrounding framework of shops, office complexes and urban apartments of WC2, was once a bog-standard car park until the Covent Garden Open Spaces Association took over in 1984. A fine job they've done too. The high red railing that encloses this site forms a decorative framework for this small park with its erratic bricked pathways that start confidently and often tail off to nowhere. Other features include shrubs, flowerbeds, arbours, wooden benches, sturdy log seating, a raised grassland area and a shed for buying plants or mugs of tea. The garden also boasts a population of frogs which have made the small grill-covered pond their home. Fruit trees and honeysuckle attract a fine variety of insects, and among the various quirky features, a dismembered stone horse's head sits Godfatheresque at the centre of a bushy plant patch. New plans for the garden include a large pond, a wildflower bank and a compost area.

Postman's Park

Area: Approx 0.5 acres
Between King Edward Street & Aldersgate Street, EC1
Tel: 020 7374 4127
Transport: St Paul's LU
Open: Daily 8am-dusk

It is the altruistic spirit of Victorian painter and philanthropist George Watts We have to thank for this commemorative green space in the heart of the City. Watt's sympathy towards the urban poor and his disdain for what he saw as the pretentiousness of the upper classes, led him to petition the Times newspaper in 1887 for a site marking the lives of ordinary 'heroic men and women', who had lost their lives saving others. This idea fell on deaf ears, so he took up the project himself and created a 50 feet long covered Heroes Wall within this former churchyard. The park gets its name from the overspill of staff from a nearby, but long demolished, postal sorting office.

These stories of selfless courage are told on hand-lettered ceramic tiles with decorative borders. Unfortunately the florid victorian prose of some of the fifty or so obituaries, in a more cynical age, read with unintentional comedy. Cases in point are inscriptions like that of 'Sarah Smith, pantomime artiste. At Prince's Theatre died of terrible injuries received when attempting in her flammable dress to extinguish the flames which had enveloped her companion. January 24 1863', or 'Ernest Bening, compositor, aged 22. Upset from a boat one dark night off Pimlico Pier grasped an oar with one hand supporting a woman with the other but sank as she was rescued. August 25 1883'. These people are heroes nonetheless, and alongside the other victims of their own good deeds, they add a particular resonance to the park.

The rest of the garden is designed with bright flowerbeds and a small fountain greeting visitors at the entrance. If you're ever stuck as to where to find this spot, it's just north of St Paul's Cathedral.

AYRES

JOHN CRANMER
CAMBRIDGE
AGED 23 A CLERK IN
THE LONDON COUNTY COUNCIL
WHO WAS DROWNED NEAR OSTEND
WHILST SAVING THE LIFE OF
A STRANGER AND A FOREIGNER
AUGUST 8 1901

G
YO
WHO
IN EN
RES
FROM I
JA

SOLOMAN G   MAN
ED 11 DIED O   RIES
1901   ING
OM   IN
EET
SAVE MYSELF"

JAMES
OF BOW
RUSHED
OPPOSITE
FIRE AND V
IN THE AT
LIFE

Postman's Park

Regent's Park

Approx 489 acres
The Store Yard, Inner Circle, Regent's Park, NW1
Tel: 020 7486 7905
Transport: Baker Street LU, Great Portland Street LU, Camden Town
LU, Regent's Park LU
Open: Daily 5am-30 mins before dusk
Facilities: Open Air Theatre, boating lake, football fields, tennis
courts, golf course, athletics track, rugby pitch, cricket pitch
Café

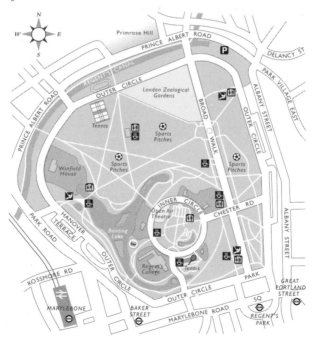

Depending on where you enter, Regent's Park is either close to Madame Tussaud's in Marylebone on its southern edge, the omnipresent gold-covered dome of the London Central Mosque to the east, and at the northern tip, Primrose Hill, which although found across the intersecting Prince Albert Road, is still included within the boundaries of the park's 487 acres. Primrose Hill famously offers far-reaching views over London's landscape, including the London Eye on the South Bank, and the TV mast of Crystal Palace, way over in SE19.

Originally known as Marylebone Park, Regent's Park was yet another 16th-century acquisition by Henry VIII for his beloved Royal Hunt. It wasn't until 1845 that Queen Victoria opened the grounds up to the public, but only for two days a week.

Made up of an inner and outer circle, Regent's Park's centre contains Queen Mary's Gardens, with wide herbaceous beds, sunken gardens, a pretty lake, rock features and a waterfall, and a rose garden. Next door, the Open Air Theatre (0870 060 1811) kicks into action every summer, with outdoor performances of Shakespearean plays including *A Midsummer Night's Dream*, family shows like *The Wind in The Willows* and *Sundays in the Park* that feature comedy and music shows. Just off the Inner Circle, a secret garden (St John's Lodge Garden) is a perfect retreat if you want a quiet stroll, as not many people use it. An arboured walkway leads to a beautifully manicured area with flowerbeds, a dramatic fountain sculpture showing Hylas being abducted by a mermaid, and the grand St John's Lodge, one of the first villas to be built in the park.

The Outer Circle, the main road that runs around the park, is two miles long and frames the larger section of the park, which includes a section of the Grand Union Canal and the 36-acre London Zoo (020 7722 3333) towards Primrose Hill. Entry to the Zoo is expensive, but it's more a conservation area than a traditional zoo, with landscaped gardens, over 600 species of animals, reptiles, birds and invertebrates, and a range of art and educational activities for children. The rest of the outer circle features a large boating lake with herons and other fine   wildfowl and wide open green areas that are dotted with deck chairs in the summer. The park is also graced with an impressive number of sports facilities – perhaps the best on offer in central London, Hyde Park being its nearest rival. Tennis and netball courts, an athletics track, cricket, football, rugby and hockey pitches are all available. The park also has four playgrounds for children – one at the foot of Primrose Hill, another by the Camden Town entrance, one by Marylebone Road, and the last close to the London Central Mosque.

Did you know?

In the 19th century, Primrose Hill was a favourite spot for duels.

Eighties pop band Madness had their photo taken on Primrose Hill for their 1982 album *The Rise and Fall*. The Rolling Stones were photographed for the cover of their *Between the Buttons* album on Primrose Hill in 1966. Oasis used Primrose Hill as a backdrop for the cover of their 1995 single, *Wonderwall*.

In January 1867, forty people drowned when the ice cracked on the lake in Regent's Park. Some time afterwards, the lake was lowered and skating forbidden.

In 1940, Prime Minister Neville Chamberlain supported a scheme to build a mosque in London. Eventually a piece of land on the western edge of Regent's Park was handed over, although the project wasn't finished until 1978.

Regent's Park

St James's Park

Area: Approx 90 acres
Between The Mall and Horse Guards Approach, SW1A
Tel: 020 7930 1793
Transport: St James's Park LU; Bus 3, 11, 12, 24, 53, 211
Open: Daily 5am-midnight
Facilities: Children's playground
Restaurant/café (Inn the Park)

Escaping from the hustle and bustle of Whitehall through Horse Guard's Parade and into this peaceful park in the heart of London is always a treat. Next door to the less elaborate Green Park, St James's Park is surrounded by three palaces. Westminster (now the Houses of Parliament) is the oldest one, then there's St James's Palace, and of course Buckingham Palace on the park's west side. Central to the area's 90 acres is the lake with its hump-backed bridge that offers views of Whitehall to the east. Swans, geese and ducks often wander from the water and waddle across the perfectly groomed lawns and around the flowerbeds. Signs warn visitors not to feed the pelicans, as there's a bit of a side show each afternoon at 3pm when park staff take to the lawns to feed these large-billed birds.

Once an expanse of marsh and meadowland, St James's Park has been through substantial changes since its establishment. The 13th century saw the land being used for a lepers hospital, which was founded by 'four leprous maidens'. In the 15th century Henry VIII acquired the land for the less philanthropic activity of deer hunting along with Hyde Park. In the mid 17th century Charles II, fresh from his exile in France, landscaped St James's in the formal French style. Even though today's park is more casual, its royal status still means cautionary signs warn against ball games, and the park is tended by a vast army of park rangers who weave in and out of the orderly troops of pedestrian tourists in their motorised green buggies. They are kept particularly busy maintaining the grand paths leading towards Buckingham Palace.

The Changing of the Guard, Trooping the Colour and Beating the Retreat are some of the royal ceremonies that draw the crowds at Horse Guards Parade. If you want to take a bit of a break from the pomp and circumstance, there's the state-of-the-art *Inn the Park* situated towards The Mall. Opened in April 2004, it's an eco-friendly building made of wood, with a turf roof and terrace (which many of the park's ducks seem to like). It has a windowed restaurant and a large self-service café for children's packed lunches, cakes and pastries.

Did you know?

In 1649, Charles I was led through St James's Park to his execution.

At one time there was a tradition that no one could be arrested in St James's Park unless the crime was very serious; but in 1677 a man called Richard Harris was sent to Bedlam for throwing an orange at King William III. Six months later, a woman called Deborah Lydall was sent to the same place for threatening to throw a stone at the Queen.

In the 18th century, cows were kept tethered in St. James's Park and visitors could buy mugs of fresh warm milk for a penny.

St James's Park

North London

Parliament Hill

Abney Park Cemetery & Nature Reserve

Area: Approx 32 acres
Stoke Newington High Street, N16
Tel: 020 7275 7557
Transport: Stoke Newington Rail; Bus 73
Open: Daily 7.30am-8pm (spring/summer)
and daily 7.30am-4pm (winter), closed 25 Dec

This Victorian park and cemetery was laid out in 1840 as one of several plots built to alleviate the overcrowding of inner city grave-yards that were struggling to cope with London's escalating population. Because the grounds were unconsecrated, the area became a favourite final resting place for Nonconformists, and eventually a thriving educational ground for nature lovers. The thirty-two acres of land are set between what was once an ancient ridgeway track – now Stoke Newington High Street – and the Hackney Brook, a stream that once ran down to the River Lea. Long gone are the 17th-century Fleetwood and Abney Houses that once stood with-in the grounds, although the decorative ironwork over the Church Street entrance to the cemetery is a remnant from Abney House. There's more ironwork over the Stoke Newington High Street entrance where the grand Egyptian gates incorporate an old lodge – now operating as a children's environmental classroom for free activities. A cobbled path leads to a ground-level sundial, which marks the start of the shrub-lined cemetery. From here the wood-land is split three ways leading to what initially looks like a gothic mess of tombstones and overgrown foliage. Amid the chaos the shrubs and trees like elms, oaks, ashes and sycamores are labelled. Those more interested in fauna will find a wonderful array of but-terflies, moths and birds - particularly in the warmer months. Paths lead to historical treasures like the raised war memorial with panels etched with the names of those who lost their lives in the two world wars. Nearby are the ruins of an old chapel. Locked up to prevent further damage, it's a weather-beaten shell that serves as a makeshift climbing frame for inquisitive children, or a landmark for others who crane their necks at the padlocked gate to admire the central spire. Guided walks and regular craft and nature activities take place in the grounds. The Abney Park Cemetery Trust offers lots of information about the cemeteries Victorian past.

Did you know?

Hackney Brook was a fair-sized stream that flowed into the River Lea. It no longer exists, but in the 19th century it formed the northern edge of Abney Park Cemetery.

Abney Park Cemetery

Alexandra Palace Park

Area: Approx 196 acres
Alexandra Palace Way, N22
Tel: 020 8365 2121
Transport: Wood Green LU, Alexandra Palace Rail;
Bus W3, 144, 184
Open: Daily 24 hours
Facilities: Alexandra Palace with indoor skating rink, children's playground, dry ski slope, boating lake
Café

Above Muswell Hill, Alexandra Palace has soldiered on despite burning down twice in 1873 and 1980. Ironically, it was built as a mini replica to the Crystal Palace glass building, which succumbed to fire in 1936. Despite such disasters, the hillside parkland that dominates the front of the building continues to thrive.

To the east of the grounds is the New River, Wood Green Reservoir and the railway line. The conservation area at the southeast entrance near Wood Green tube station, was once used as a rifle range, and also made up part of an old racecourse. It's now a five acre area of meadow and woodland, with a large number of oaks some dating back three hundred years to when Tottenham Wood was still in existence. Elms, holly and chestnut trees also stake out their territory here. The start of the Parkland Walk Footpath is over on the west side of the grounds. The route leads to Finsbury Park, taking in Queen's Wood and Highgate Wood along the way.

Behind the Palace, the boating lake opens in the summer and caters for those who want to try out the rowing or pedal boats, but it's a bit of a scruffy watering hole, despite the ducks and geese that still use it. Beside the lake is the animal enclosure, where donkeys and deer are often startled by daytime foxes. Apparently, some cats that have snubbed domesticity and turned feral can also be seen on the hunt for one of the many brown rats and woodland mice that flourish here.

Bruce Castle Park

Area: Approx 196 acres
Lordship Lane, N17
Tel: 020 8808 8772
Open: Daily 24 hours
Transport: Wood Green LU then bus 243; Seven Sisters LU/Rail then bus 123, 243; Bruce Grove Rail
Facilities: Children's playground, tennis court, bowling green

The Green Flag-awarded Bruce Castle Park surrounds the Bruce Castle Museum, a 16th-century manor house at the eastern end of Lordship Lane. The grounds are what remain of the ancient Bruce family estate, which may well have had a castle as far back as 1086.

A central point of interest within the park is the magnificent ancient oak – said to be around 400 years old – that sits near the children's playground. The play area itself has two significant dips in the ground that are said to be the remnants of a medieval fishpond, which also hints at the area's past. Just beyond the main entrance on Lordship Lane, a tall turreted redbrick tower beside the museum dates from the early 1500s. There's a sealed entrance to its basement, and a window high up on the south side, which can be better seen from inside the park. Other historical features are an octagonal stone slab just north of the museum, which marks the spot where a drinking fountain was placed in 1893 by the British Women's Temperance Association to encourage people to keep off the beer.

Today, tennis courts and a paddling pool (open May to August) bring in a decent amount of people, as does the annual Bruce Castle multicultural festival (June). Well-manicured lawns and features like pretty flowerbeds next to the bowling green have surely contributed to the park's award-winning status, although the enclosed Holocaust Garden of Remembrance stands out as a poignant addition to the grounds. Opened in January 2001 (National Holocaust Memorial Day), this circular garden offers a peaceful space for contemplation, and has benches, rock features and tall hedges, and honours those who have died through holocaust, genocide and atrocities. If you visit the garden or the main park, it's likely that you'll be tempted towards the free museum (open 1-5pm Wed to Sun), which offers weekend and holiday children's activities and holds the entire collections of the borough of Haringey.

Natural Park

Camley Street Natural Park

Area: Approx 2 acres
12 Camley Street, NW1
Tel: 020 7833 2311
Transport: King's Cross LU/Rail
Open: Mon-Thurs 9am-5pm (summer) and 9am-dusk (winter),
weekends 11am-5pm (summer) and 10am-4pm (winter)

A perfect respite from the urban chaos and redevelopment of the King's Cross area, Camley Street Natural Park offers a haven for Londoners with a thirst for some natural green space. Managed by the London Wildlife Trust, the reserve runs parallel with a section of the Regent's Canal and footpath. Once a derelict site, it was originally used for coal storage during the Victorian era. It opened to the public in 1985 and has a visitor centre at the entrance, with a workshop area for children, while the park – most of which is wheelchair accessible – offers a patchwork of meadow, coppice, woodland and pond areas, all tended by hardworking staff.

A lush variety of plantlife exists throughout, with trees including silver birches, hazels and rowans doing a good job of obscuring the greater part of the urban surroundings. It's when you stand at the upper point of the woodland paths that you get a full reminder of the gritty NW1 landscape. Otherwise, this is a perfect retreat for spotting frogs, newts and toads in the damp marshy areas, or grasshoppers and butterflies in the wildflower meadow. Children are consistently drawn here by the opportunity to check out the 'mini beast hotel' a small pond that attracts everything from ladybirds to grubs, larvae and spiders. There are also special education programmes for local schools and groups that run during term time and need to be booked.

Environmentally themed activities run throughout the year, with £1 donations suggested for events like Tree Dressing days, Wildlife Watches and hands-on conservation workshops – though it's the pond dipping that's often the most popular with leeches, flatworms and sticklebacks to be found.

Clissold Park

Area: Approx 53 acres
Stoke Newington Church Street, N16
Tel: 020 8923 3660
Transport: Stoke Newington Rail; Bus 73, 149, 329, 476
Open: Daily 7.30am-dusk
Facilities: Children's playground & paddling pool, football and cricket pitches, tennis courts, zoo
Café

Along with Hackney's two other historical parks (Abney Park Cemetery and Springfield Park), Clissold's layout, features and architecture have awarded it Grade II listing status. Set in the grounds of an 18th-century house, it was once known as Crawshaw Farm before opening up as a public space in 1889. Its 53 acres stretch from Green Lanes to the west, Queen Elizabeth's Close to the north and Stoke Newington Church Street to the south-east. A particular landmark is Clissold House (now a café), with its surrounding rose garden and outdoor tables in the summer. This site overlooks a Victorian cast-iron footbridge, built over the intermittent water flow of a section of the New River. The park's other features include avenues of ash, lime, oak and plane trees, as well as two adjacent ponds to the north, with a resting island for the herons, swans, kestrels and ducks. There are even more feathered species in the park's aviary, which houses quails, love birds and budgies, all providing a vibrantly shrill medley of lime greens, royal blues, bright yellow and orange hues. Fallow deer are found in their own enclosure, and the next door zoo (which can look a bit deserted) has notices warning against feeding the animals, with a few paunchy, and apparently arthritic goats as evidence of some former largesse.

A children's playground, summer paddling pool and cricket and football pitches provide facilities for active types, and the tennis courts here are home to the Hackney branch of the City Tennis Centre (020 8318 4856), where all ages can book for classes.

Stoke Newington Festival – Clissold Park

Finsbury Park

Area: Approx 115 acres
Endymion Road, N4
Tel: 020 8802 9139/020 8489 5694
Transport: Finsbury Park LU/Rail
Open: Daily dawn til dusk
Facilities: Children's playground, athletics track, gym, cricket pitch
Clubs: London Heathside Runners (020 8802 9139),
London Capitals Youth American Football Club (020 8265 1156)
Café

Perhaps best known for hosting the annual Irish Fleadh music festival, the FinFest and other notable celebrations, the sprawl of green land that makes up Finsbury Park has existed in London for centuries. The park dates from around 1869, but it lies on the site of the ancient forest of Middlesex, and shares some of the original boundaries. Features from the mid 19th century are the grand gated entrances, the lake and island, and a modest number of willows, poplars, and oaks. Currently undergoing regeneration as part of a major project that covers the whole Finsbury Park area, there's a definite sense of much-needed development.

The southern entrance to the park from Finsbury Park station slopes up from Manor House and Seven Sisters. It's all a bit sparse until you get up the lake and boathouse. The site of much urban planning, the lake has remained unchanged since the 1860s. At the beginning of 2004 it was dredged to allow for further happy breeding of the ducks and geese in their new oxygenated habitat. It's the current work-a-day café and children's area in sight of the lake that are due for the most changes. With regeneration work set to run up until 2006, a new enclosed playground with extra swings and a 'castle' mound is planned, as well as a grand conservatory-style café overlooking the water. Further park improvements will include new shelters, fencing, footpaths and gardens, but there are still established features to be proud of in the community nursery, horticultural centre and neat flower garden not far from the lake. At the heart of the park is the athletics track, where American football teams play and train. The park also has a gym open seven days a week. Things get a bit greener and pleasanter beyond the sports arena, with sloping lawns framed by trees leading down to the cricket pitch (admittedly fairly shabby), and the far more interesting path of the New River aqueduct. Opened in 1613 to bring fresh water from Hertfordshire to London, Thames Water still uses it as a source for London's drinking water. The route provides a 25 mile long footpath. There's no public access to the river, but it flows beyond Finsbury Park and ends at the Stoke Newington West reservoir.

Did you know?

Finsbury Park, which opened in 1869, was not within the parish of Finsbury. Its location on the old site of Hornsey Wood was the closest open area that could be found for the urbanised Finsbury residents.

Hampstead Heath

Area: Approx 800 acres
Between West Heath Road and Highgate West Hill, NW5
Tel: 020 7485 4491
Transport: Kentish Town LU, Gospel Oak or Hampstead Heath Rail;
Bus 214, C2, C11
Open: Daily dawn til dusk
Facilities: Swimming ponds and lido, fishing ponds, cricket pitches,
football and rugby pitches, golf putting greens, horse-riding circuit,
model boating lake, tennis courts, bowling green
Cafés and Restaurant (see map for details)

Take your pick from the meadow, lawns, valleys, flowerbeds and woodlands all found within this 800 acre heath that sits on the hill above Hampstead Heath station and adds to the area's village-like character. Famous for its ponds – there are around 30 of them – the best known ones are the six largest, two of which are restricted to single sex bathing. The general look of the heath is deliberately unkempt. A mixture of woodland and meadow, much of the open land is left unmown to give it a rough and natural look. In the summer months there is long dry hay in some areas with none of the sheep from bygone years to graze on it.

Stretching across two boroughs (Camden and Barnet), Hampstead Heath is a vast green area, hosting regular large scale events like cross country runs of heath-based groups like the Highgate Harriers, who train at the Parliament Hill Athletics track. The Hampstead Rugby Football Club and the London Orienteering Klubb (LOK) both use the heath for training. Parliament Hill is a favourite location for kite flyers, who can catch the best winds and also take in the excellent views of the yawning miles of the city from here. Down towards Gospel Oak railway station, the Lido is a good option for family swimming if you want to bypass the segregated areas of the ponds – although it does get very crowded on fine days. Tennis courts, a running track, bandstand and bowling green are also not far from the station.

There have been a few historical attempts to re-style the heath. Back in the 1850s, there were plans to turn the area into a parkland, with a few earnest efforts to lay brickwork and remove the then characteristic areas of sand and gravel, but the project soon floundered. During the Second World war sand was taken from the heath, although this was to fill sand bags from the relentless bombing raids rather than to remodel the heath. The vacant pits left dotted throughout the landscape were later filled with rubble from blitzed out sites around London.

Today a burial mound at the edge of one of the meadows is listed as an archaeological monument. Said by some to be a Bronze Age barrow, the British Museum in 1894 unearthed a top layer of 'modern rubbish'. Whatever its origin, the site is now enclosed by a fence, with a few benches providing good views towards the east end of London and the River Thames.

The northern edge of the heath is a good place for picnickers who can lounge in the grounds of the elegant Robert Adam designed Kenwood House. It's from here that the valley slopes down to the ponds. The Kenwood open air stage has summer concerts, and the house offers tours of the Iveagh Bequest – a collection of paintings by artists including Van Dyck, Reynolds and Rembrandt. It also serves snacks year round.

Children and families swarm to Golders Hill Park on the far eastern edge of the heath, where the café selling excellent ice-cream does a roaring trade during the hottest months.

Did you know?

In Bram Stoker's 1837 novel *Dracula*, children are found on Hampstead Heath with 'tiny wounds in the throat'.

Kenwood House in Hampstead Heath was used as a location for the 1999 film *Notting Hill* starring Hugh Grant and Julia Roberts.

GOLDERS GREEN

Sports
Pitches

HAMPSTEAD WAY

WILDWOOD ROAD

NORTH END ROAD

WEST HEATH AV.

HAMPSTEAD WAY

Tennis

Golders Hill Park

NORTH END WAY

Sandy
Heath

SPANIARDS ROAD

The
Elms

West Heath

Inverforth
House

East Hea

P

WEST HEATH ROAD

Pond

Vale of Heath

N
W   E
S

BRANCH HILL

LOWER TER.

HEATH STREET

EAST HEAT

WELL WALK

NEW END SQ.

HAMPSTEAD

HEATH STREET

FLASK WALK

WIL

HAMPSTEAD HIGH ST.

44

HAMPSTEAD LANE

th Wood

Kenwood House

Kenwood
(nglish Heritage)

Concert
Site

Dueling
Ground

**South
Meadow**

FITZROY PARK

Ponds

MILLFIELD LANE

Sports
Pitches

Ponds

**Parliament
Hill Fields**

HIGHGATE ROAD

Parliament Hill

Bowling
Green
Tennis

Ponds

SOUTH HILL PARK

PARLIAMENT HILL

P

Athletics
Track

Sports
Pitches

Lido

P

cher's
ill
OAD

SOUTH END ROAD

HAMPSTEAD HEATH

SAVERNAKE ROAD

GOSPEL OAK

Highgate Wood and Queen's Wood

Area: Approx 70 acres
Muswell Hill Road, N10
Tel: 020 8444 6129
Transport: Highgate LU; Bus 43, 134, 263
Open: Daily 7.30am til dusk
Facilities: Football & cricket pitches, playground, information centre
Café

Long live Highgate Wood, whose seventy acres were once part of the old forest of Middlesex, but are said to date even further back to the last ice age. Located north of Highgate tube, the woods today are generally an area of conservation with nature trails, a children's playground and spaces for picnics and ballgames. This is also a popular destination for those looking for great food with The Pavilion café, serving delicious organic fare in a pretty garden framed by rhododendron bushes and rosebeds.

Owned by the Corporation of London, the woods have been generally well tended since 1886 and were awarded a green flag along with Hampstead Heath. Vast oaks and hornbeams are the most common trees within the grounds, but there's also ample eyecandy by way of the swathes of bluebells that cover much of the ground during the spring. Some parts of the wood are fenced off to allow for further growth of the shrublands, and visitors with a deeper yen for nature can take part in organised wildlife walks or trails that reveal many old and new plant species, the populations of over 70 species of birds, five species of bat, 20 types of butterfly and an awesome 100 species of spider.

Highgate Wood is a busy place throughout the year with seasonal activities including stories beside the Story-telling-Tree, Christmas tree recycling at the beginning of every year, and beetle safaris which focus on the 454 spottable species here. Children can have fun in the award-winning playground, whose bridge and tower features are both wheelchair and buggy accessible. The area also has signs and noticeboards written in Braille.

Across the Muswell Hill Road is the 52 acre Queen's Wood, which has also been awarded for its landscape. With less attention given to it by staff, it's a denser option that preserves a far more natural woodland environment than its larger neighbour. Back in the 19th century, it was known as Churchyard Bottom Wood, due to the unearthing of a human burial pit from the Great Plague of 1665. It's current name refers to Queen Victoria. These days, thanks to the huge storm of 1987, the natural felling of trees means that a tad more sunlight is able to seep through the woodland. There's a stream at the northern end of the grounds, and visitors can join the Parkland Walk Footpath – a four mile route than runs along north London's disused railway lines from Finsbury Park to Alexandra Palace via Highgate.

Queen's Park

Queens Park

Area: Approx 30 acres
Kingswood Avenue, NW6
Tel: 020 8969 5661
Transport: Queen's Park LU/Rail
Open: Daily 7.30am-dusk
Facilities: Farm, tennis courts, playground, pitch and putt
Café

This park comes as a quiet antidote to the bustling High Road of NW6. One of the Corporation of London's vast collection of well maintained green spaces, the park was used as part of the 1879 Royal Kilburn Agricultural Show that was graced by the presence of Queen Victoria. Her title was attached to the park in honour of her Golden Jubilee. Today, the park's 30 acres are designed to give visitors a space in which to exercise, play or relax. The Quiet Garden at the Queen's Park Station entrance on Harvist Road is designated as a restful area and is a bit more formal than the rest of the park, it's manicured lawns skilfully interspersed with vivid flowerbeds, bushes, hedgerows and benches along the path. Next to this garden is a small farm where children are always happy to look at (or handle) the chickens, turkeys, rabbits and goats. For more raucous activity, there's a children's playground over on the park's west side.

A Sensory Garden in the park's centre has a water feature, wind-chimes and fragrant plants for further peaceful contemplation. Sports are available on the tennis courts and the pitch and putt field, and a listed bandstand offers a summer programme of music events.

Nature calls in the Woodland Walk area which is located in the park's north-east corner, where wildflowers, frogs, toads, insects, foxes and hedgehogs can all be spotted. There are numbered posts throughout the area to help explain all the different features.

West London

Bishop's Park

Area: Approx 27 acres
Bishop's Avenue, SW6
Tel: 020 7736 7181
Transport: Putney Bridge, East Putney, Parson's Green and Fulham Broadway LU
Open: Daily 7.30am-dusk
Facilities: Paddling pool, bowling pavilion, tennis courts and pavilion, playground
Café

Bishop's Park is excellent for river views as it runs alongside the Thames Path, which looks out towards Putney Bridge. It is also a good vantage point for the start of the annual Oxford vs Cambridge boat race. Opened in 1893, the park contains Fulham Palace and its beautiful grounds, and follows (as closely as possible) the historical line of a moat that once enclosed the palace from around AD 704. This trail is marked out by circular landmarks on easily accessible paths that take in the park's ancient earthworks, the Palace and its gateways, the Thames, allotments (a hotchpotch of cultivated meadow land), moat gardens (ornamental trees shrubs and a rockery), an ice house and a wilderness area behind the moat garden – which is a haven for wildlife, shrubs and oak trees. The trail should take just under an hour to complete, but could easily take a lot longer if you have the time to spare. Another interesting site is the small Spanish Memorial Garden between the famous All Saints Church at the edge of Putney Bridge, and a secluded Rose Garden close by the Thames Path. Set on a raised area that provides a good view of the river, the memorial features a plaque for members of the International Brigade who left Hammersmith and Fulham to fight Franco's forces during the Spanish Civil War.

Emslie Horniman Pleasance

Area: Approx 3 acres
Bosworth Road, W10
Tel: 020 7471 9813
Transport: Westbourne Park LU/Rail
Open: Daily dawn til dusk
Facilities: Multi sports astro pitch, children's playground
Kiosk (spring & summer only)

The south London based Horniman Society donated this park to the west London area in the mid 19th century, and architect Charles Voysey was brought in to landscape the site. His name lives on here in the enclosed Spanish-style Voysey garden in the far corner of the park. Laid out at the back of the kiosk, it's a white walled area with a mini sunken moat, herb borders, flowerbeds and a pergola for climbing plants. It's only accessible with the permission of the park warden. That said, it's a beautiful spot, even if you're unlucky enough to have to view it from the luscious borders that surround it.

In 1998 the park's main areas underwent a considerable refurbishment the benefits of which can be seen today. It has a large and traditional looking adventure playground, while all other areas display an excellent use of diverse contemporary materials in a natural setting. Bright metal pillars and artworks, raised and cobbled flowerbeds, a floodlit hard play area and a large multicoloured enclosed children's playground are all part of the refurbishment. The park is overlooked by the high rise Trellick Tower and nearby is Meanwhile Gardens. A nice touch within Emslie Horniman Pleasance is the circular and peaceful sunken 'Quiet Garden', with heavy duty stone and wooden benches, rock seating and cobblestones etched with moralistic missives like 'loving words are more powerful than a big stick'. Although the park is relatively small, it has been lovingly preserved for the local community, and is also used for annual events. The steel pan drumming festival in the lead up to the Notting Hill carnival is held here, and the park also serves as a VIP zone for special visitors during the carnival itself.

Emslie Horniman Pleasance

Fulham Palace Botanical Gardens

Area: Approx 16 acres
Bishop's Avenue (off Fulham Palace Road), SW6
Tel: 020 7736 3223
Transport: Hammersmith or Putney Bridge LU; Bus 220, 414, 430
Open: Daily 24 hours

Fulham Palace Botanical Gardens are set within the surrounding grounds of Bishop's Park, but were separated from the larger grounds in the late 19th century. They form a pretty enclosure for Fulham Palace, and so deserve a mention of their own. The Fulham Palace site is a Scheduled Ancient Monument, while the surrounding botanical park is Grade II English Heritage listed – unlike any other green space in the borough. There are usually tours of the grounds and museum by the Palace curator, although recent Lottery-funded refurbishment has disturbed this arrangement (check for re-opening details).

The botanical garden consists of an open lawn at the back of the Palace building and is edged by magnolias, shrubs and woodland paths. In a far corner is a 500 year old oak, with a huge trunk carrying a large split, which explains the thick supporting plank that keeps it upright. An original red-brick wall at the far edge of the lawn surrounds a kitchen garden. It can be entered though a small Tudor gate, or from an alternative side entrance found along a tree-lined path to the left.

Once inside you'll be hit with the pungent aroma of up to twenty herbs including lemon balm, lavender, thyme, sage and sorrel. The many bushes, shrubs, and a meadow area make this a pretty and often quiet spot. To help visitors navigate their way around, all areas are numbered on a map inside the Tudor gate. In the far distance towards the south, you can see the flag-topped turrets of the medieval tower of All Saint's Church, which sits at the Putney Bridge end of Bishop's Park.

Gunnersbury Park

Area: 186 acres
Popes Lane, Acton, W3
Tel: 020 8992 1612
Transport: Acton Town LU, Kew Bridge Rail (10 min walk); Bus E3
Open: Daily dawn til dusk
Facilities: Children's playgrounds, boating and fishing lake, bowling green, tennis courts, lacrosse pitch, football and rugby pitches
Café

Gunnersbury Park was for many centuries part of the estate of the Bishops of London, before falling into private ownership. A grand house was built here in the early 19th century, designed by John Webb, which served as the home for Princes Amelia – George II's favourite daughter – between 1763 and her death in 1786. Although the original house was destroyed in 1801, much of the landscaping and several of the park's features date from Princess Amelia's residency. The house and lands went through several owners before Alexander Copland bought the land and built the large Georgian house that stands here today. It was acquired by Nathan Rothschild in 1835 and remained as a family estate until sold to the boroughs of Ealing and Acton in 1925.

The large and leafy park that stands here today has been in existence since 1926, but has lost little of its former glory with many original features such as a boating lake, several ponds, orangery, Italian gardens, mock gothic ruin and a neo-classical temple. These ornate features are complemented by acres of open space with plenty of mature trees. Those looking for sport rather than relaxation will also find plenty to do here with a miniature golf course, tennis courts, football, lacrosse and rugby pitches, a boating and fishing lake and bowling green. The park also has two playgrounds for those seeking to keep kids entertained. Gunnersbury Park has the usual selection of park wildlife, but has a particularly varied selection of wildfowl. The fine stucco house has become a local museum which is worth a visit.

Hammersmith Park

Area: Approx 7 acres
South Africa Road, W12
Tel: 020 7736 1735/020 8748 3020
Transport: White City LU
Open: Daily 7.30am until dusk
Facilities: Bowling green, sandpit and paddling pool, playground and tennis courts

A neat and tidy neighbourhood park behind the White City Estate and close to the complex of Queen's Park Rangers Football Club. The biggest draw of this linear landscape is its central garden and lake. The park's two entrances lead up to this central site, Frithville Gardens, which backs onto a few industrial buildings, and the more open main entrance at South Africa Road. The later offers a picturesque promenade of benches and rosebeds, as well as a gated paddling pool, tennis courts and a play area.

Back to the central garden, which is built in a Japanese style, complete with stone lanterns, a stone basin, a cobbled path. Rugged steps lead up to the two stone viewing benches at its highest point, which overlook a humpbacked bridge over the lake. There are usually fountains providing an aquatic display, but this depends on the season. The lush surroundings include lovingly planted bushes, trees, bamboo grasses, azaleas and japanese holly.

The park lies on land that is one of the few remaining remnants of the great White City Franco-British Exhibition of 1907. This was a dazzling 140 acre stretch of pavilions, courts and decorative domes all built in white stucco. The site was later used for the fourth Olympic Games of 1908.

Holland Park

Area: Approx 54 acres
Ilchester Place, W8
Tel: 020 7471 9813
Transport: Holland Park LU
Open: Daily 7.30am-dusk
Facilities: Cricket pitch, youth hostel, theatre
Café

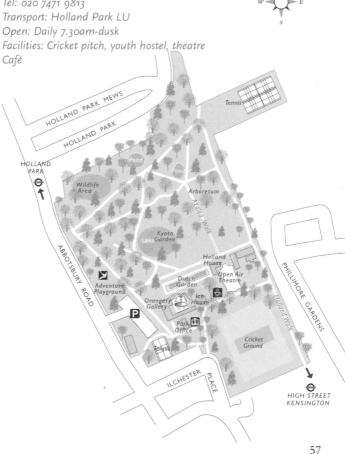

Holland Park is the largest green space in the well-healed Royal Borough of Kensington and Chelsea, and is surrounded by grand residential mansion houses. There are several landmark buildings in the area that are open to the public for guided tours such as the house of Victorian cartoonist Linley Sambourne, and Leighton House – the former home of artist Frederick Lord Leighton. Central to the park are the murals and terraces that are all that remains of Holland House that was bombed out during the Second World War. During the summer this site is used as the venue for open-air theatre.

Most people tend to flock to the Japanese Garden with its Koi carp filled pond and central fountain. The sloping woodlands that surround the park are good for spotting squirrels, peacocks, and a further fifty or so species of birds that have been found here over the last decade. Crows, jays, robins and magpies are regular visitors, and long-eared bats can be seen near the ponds during dusk, or hovering around the slightly forlorn statue of a seated Lord Holland who surveys his own pond at the edge of a woodland path. For more details about the wildlife in the park the Ecology Centre (020 7471 9809) has maps, nets for pond dipping and is a great source of information.

Those more interested in star spotting than bird spotting will often find otherwise rare migratory creatures such as Jade Jagger strolling along a path. This park being the closest green space for the models, actors and pop stars that live in Notting Hill and the surrounding area. To cater for such visitors Holland Park has an excellent café and a conservatory-style Orangery which is used for weddings, parties and exhibitions. The numerous Parks Police and special dog toilets show how seriously the maintenance of the parks lawns and gardens are taken.

Active sports activities include football and cricket, as well as five-week jogging programmes for beginners. The netball course for those nostalgic for their schooldays and year-round power-walking sessions can all be booked by calling 020 7471 9816.

Holland Park

Meanwhile Gardens

Area: Approx 4 acres
156-158 Kensal Road, W10
Tel: 020 8960 4600
Transport: Westbourne Park or Westbourne Grove LU/Rail
Open: Daily
Facilities: Skate bowl

This community garden was set up in the 1970s to offset the concrete surrounds of W10. Overshadowed by the gigantic Trellick Tower, it's a linear strip of land running from the residential estates of Kensal Road to the Carlton Bridge steps leading up to Westbourne Park Road. The garden extends along a section of the Grand Union Canal, where cyclists and walkers share the open pathway, and west London residents can be seen on the opposite side throwing bread down for the wildfowl. Inside the park, enjoyable features include the wildlife garden and boardwalks, allotment area, herb-scented courtyard and duck pond, which are all at the Kensal Road end. The path towards Westbourne Park includes cobbled walkways, meadowland, a free play hut for under-6's, a popular graffitied skate bowl and a modest area of sloping parkland below the west London traffic.

Ravenscourt Park

Area: Approx 30 acres
Ravenscourt Road, W6
Tel: 020 8748 3020
Transport: Ravenscourt Park LU
Open: Daily 7.30am-dusk
Facilities: Children's playgrounds, basketball nets, tennis courts, bowling green, football pitch
Café

An ordered expanse of open land in a fairly well-heeled area of London, Ravenscourt Park has a history that goes back to 1888. Back then, Ravenscourt House (at the Paddenswick Road entrance), once rivalled the grand pile of Fulham Palace in providing second residence for the Bishop of London. The building crumbled under bombing in 1941, and now a scented walled garden blossoms in its place. Neatly-sculpted topiary, lively flowerbeds and serene communal seating are all beautifully arranged here, thanks to the green-fingered loyalty of volunteers. In the other areas of the main park, the prettiest spot is beside the tree-lined lake, which is best viewed from the humpbacked bridge that straddles it. Framed by willows, bushes and populated by ducks, coots, swans and mallards, it's also surrounded by pristine flowerbeds, some of which have been planted specifically for film shoots. It's worth stopping by at the popular Ravenscourt Park Teahouse, a stone's throw from the lake. Here, snacks, sweets or full blown hot or cold meals can be eaten inside the café or at the outside tables. Either way, this family-friendly enclave might have you feeling strangely conspicuous if you're not actively nursing, cajoling or scolding a child. Aside from these areas, the rest of the 30 acre park is an easily walkable area of flat green land, with designated dog exercise areas, an astro-turfed football pitch, four separate tennis courts, a bowling green and no less than three children's play areas.

South-west London

Battersea Park

Area: Approx 200 acres
Between Albert Bridge Road and Queenstown Road, SW11
Tel: 020 8871 7530
Transport: Battersea Park or Queenstown Road Rail,
Sloane Square LU; Bus 19, 137
Open: Daily 7am-dusk
Facilities: Millennium sports arena, all weather pitches,
children's zoo, tennis courts, cycle hire, fishing lake
Café

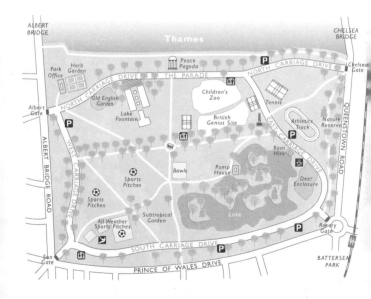

There are a multitude of features in this inner city park that's arranged in a series of circular carriageways around a grand central bandstand. With 200 acres of land split into lush gardens (Old English, Herb, Rose, Sub-Tropical and Winter), mounds of well-designed flowerbeds, exotic trees, open lawns and playgrounds; there's something for everyone here. A key attraction is the large fishing lake with open or dense shrub, bush or fern-lined edges. A Barbara Hepworth sculpture called 'Single Form' is situated between the lake and the south carriage drive. Henry Moore also gets a look in with his three stone female figures, which overlook the lake's north side, south of the central carriageway.

Battersea Park was the site of the 1951 Festival of Britain Pleasure Gardens, which had a permanent funfair that rolled along until the early 1970s, by which time the park seemed to lose its lustre. Large-scale renovations took place throughout 2003, resulting in new features, including the fountain area just below the Carriage Drive North. The fountain is impressive with jets of up to fifteen feet and low metal barriers to keep excitable children from diving in. The adjacent rose garden is a well-landscaped area that seems to inspire visitors with yoga mats, or those practising Tai Chi. On Carriage Drive North itself, the huge Thameside Peace Pagoda is perhaps the park's best-known landmark. Three-tiers tall, with panels showing a preaching, sleeping or contemplating Buddha, you can take to its steps for panoramic views of the Thames and both Chelsea and Albert bridges. The structure was built in 1985 by Japanese monks and nuns in memory of Hiroshima Day, and to encourage world peace. It's along this area's wide Thameside path that you'll often see the hired bikes, tandems and low yellow tricycles from London Recumbents (020 7498 6543) being ridden by adults and children. The park's Battersea Children's Zoo (020 8871 7540) soldiers defiantly on, despite regular funding problems. For sports, the Battersea Park Millennium Arena (020 8871 7537) has nineteen floodlit tennis courts, an all-weather sports pitch, a running track and a fitness centre.

Battersea Park

Streatham Rookery

Area: Approx 4 acres
Covington Way, Streatham Common, SW16
Tel: 020 8764 4079
Transport: Streatham Common, Streatham Rail;
Bus 50, 60, 109, 118, 159, 249, 255
Open: Daily 9am-4.45 pm
Facilities: Tennis court, basketball court, football pitch
Café (outside the Gardens)

Streatham is a designated conservation area with 70 acres of green space that includes Streatham Common, which stretches from the main high street and up towards Norwood. However, many people in and around SW16 are unaware of the walled Rookery, a peaceful and well-kept series of circular gardens found within the highest point of the common. Two entrances next to the main car park reveal the four acre gardens, where the main bench-lined path offers an expansive view beyond the gardens and over towards Norwood Grove★. Steps within the Rookery lead down to each separate 'garden room', which include an *Old English Garden*, *Ornamental Garden*, tennis court, picnic area and orchard and the *White Garden* – an oblong-shaped space with six white benches, and all-white flowering plants.

The gardens are framed by narrow sloping paths, either cobbled or smooth, with surrounding bushes. The arboured walkways look particularly good in the summer, and even during hot weather, the Rookery never gets particularly crowded, which adds to its sense of being a secret garden. Features like a pillared sundial, a mini pond and water fountain, large cedars, fern trees and even the occasional outdoor theatre event make the whole Rookery experience something that many of Streatham's locals probably want to keep to themselves. One particular point of interest is a central wishing well – originally one of three – which marks the site of the ancient mineral wells that Streatham was famous for in the 17th and 18th centuries.

The Rookery didn't open as a public park until 1913, when it formed the grounds of a large house that was demolished during the early 1900s. However its history, which is very much linked with Streatham's waters, goes back to 1659 when agricultural labourers freshened up at the spring here, and made elaborate claims for the effects of the waters that were said to cure everything from rheumatism to gout or blindness. No wonder then, that the site was developed as a medicinal spa with coaches and crowds often queuing for a mile along Streatham High Road to get into the grounds.

Nearby local nature reserves:

Eardley Road Sidings *(Bates Crescent, SW16, off Abercairn Road and Greyhound Lane)*

Unigate Wood *(Namba Roy Close, SW16, off Valley Road)*

Norwood Grove* *(Covington Way, SW16)* A large park adjacent to Streatham Common, with formal gardens and wooded areas. Norwood Grove Mansion is in the park and is set in its own ornamental gardens.

Vauxhall Park

Area: Approx 8.5 acres
Lawn Lane, SW8
Tel: 020 7926 9000
Open: Daily dawn til dusk
Transport: Vauxhall LU/Rail; Bus 2, 88
Facilities: Children's playground, tennis courts, basketball court

Something's been happening to Vauxhall Park over the last few years. This modest Victorian park, which borders South Lambeth Road and Fentiman Road, has been undergoing a few pleasing changes. The underused green lawn at the Fentiman Road entrance has now been morphed into a thriving lavender garden. A confident sea of lilac leads to the rose arbor – another pretty spot offering its best colour from spring to autumn. Two tennis courts and a basketball court are regularly used facilities, although the disused toilet blocks and a shabby One O'clock Club building are in line for future refurbishment. A mix and match of themes within the park include a Victorian fountain with cascading water, a grand cast iron entrance and 'unfinished' walkway to the enclosed children's play area and picnic lawn. There is also a model village nestling among fir trees and flowerbeds, with banks of bijou thatched cottages – all courtesy of the Friends of Vauxhall Park. There are plans to develop the children's playground with updated climbing equipment and swings for children up to twelve years old, as well as a new sand and water area.

Windmill Gardens

Area: Approx 1.3 acres
Blenheim Gardens, Brixton, SW2
Transport: Brixton LU/Rail; Bus 159, 109, 133, 59, 118
Open: Daily 24 hours

Tucked away behind the Blenheim Gardens Studios and estates of Brixton Hill is this SW2 park and archaeological site. A compact green space with a One O'clock Club and children's play area, this little garden is best known for the old Brixton Windmill. The windmill stands 12 metres tall, and was built in 1816 when SW2 was nothing but open fields. It was a working mill right up to the early 20th century, and is the only one to have survived of 12 other sites that have been identified in Lambeth. It is now a Grade II listed building. Made with eighteen-inch thick brickwork, it pretty much dominates the landscape, particularly with its black colouring, which mirrors the original tar that protected it from the elements.

South-east London

Crystal Palace Park

Brockwell Park

Area: Approx 128 acres
Between Dulwich Road and Norwood Road, SE24
Tel: 020 7926 0105
Transport: Brixton LU/Rail then buses 2, 3, 37, 196 or Herne Hill Rail
Open: Park daily 7am-dusk; Lido (June to September) Mon-Fri
6.45am-8pm; Sat & Sun 12noon-6pm
Facilities: Olympic-sized Lido, Sure Start, One O'clock Club and chil-
dren's playground, tennis courts, football pitch, basketball court,
bowling green and badminton court
Brixton Beach Café and Brockwell Hall Café

The sloping grounds of Brockwell Park first opened to the public in 1892. Formerly a private estate, it's bordered by Tulse Hill, Norwood and Herne Hill/Brixton. An expansive arena, its dimensions are big enough for the park to feel perennially underpopulated, even in the summer when its grassy slopes are pleasantly dotted with dedicated sunseekers. It's only when the annual festivals roll into town that any real crowds start to gather. Once the host site of Gay Pride, the park now contents itself with the Jayday Cannabis Festival (late May or early June), the two-day Lambeth Country Show (July), an annual fireworks display (November) and a succession of funfairs and circuses throughout the year.

Perhaps Brockwell's best hidden gem is the beautiful walled rose garden, its gate located just beyond a small white porticoed shelter that was once a private chapel, but is now a public loo. Inside the garden, wooden benches are placed among the shrubs and seasonally changing flowers, and an overriding sense of serenity makes this an excellent spot for quiet contemplation. Permanent features include an old mulberry tree and a lush array of well-coiffed box and yew hedges. There's also an old well inside the entrance that's covered by grating, and a sundial suspended from the wall in the far corner – though it's often swamped by a mass of wisteria. For a less manicured dip into nature, the nearby community garden centre is where volunteers have transformed what was once a derelict fly tip into a haven for fruit and vegetables. Visitors are welcome on open days where plants like organic kitchen herbs are on sale in the greenhouses. Other pleasures within the main park are the willow and oak lined duck ponds. These miniature lakes are separated by a small humpbacked bridge, and have been spruced up and reshaped in recent years. This has resulted in even more in the way of Canada geese, mallards and mute swans, and less of the water rats that took some of the joy out of a stroll by the water.

For leisure pursuits, the tennis courts, football pitch, bowling green and basketball court draw in the locals. The Brockwell Youth Cup, which is battled over by soccer-mad Lambeth schools, has been running here annually since 2001. However, the park is probably most famous for its 1930s Olympic-sized Lido, which opens from June to September. Known as Brixton Beach, the pool has been under persistent threat of closure, but still soldiers defiantly on with a loyal following of early morning or late night dippers, who brave the cold water. These hardy folk refuel with snacks and occasional themed barbecues at the poolside Brixton Beach Café. Although the pool is closed during the winter months, a yoga room offers tai chi, meditation, Balinese energy and pregnancy yoga sessions for adults in search of the feelgood factor, while children can express themselves in the Whippersnapper music and performance classes. There's also circus skills and acrobatics with the Mighty Wanderer whose workshops take place during term times (020 7738 6633).

A relatively new addition to the Brockwell grounds is the model railway. Usually attracting a small audience, it was built in 2003 at the personal expense of rail enthusiasts Roland Baker and Derek Hoare. The £1 rides take children on a 220 yard round trip from the park's Herne Hill entrance to the side of the Lido complex. However, if you and yours are set on walking, all upward leading paths take you to the brow of the steepest hill. It is here that the Grade II listed Brockwell Hall – now the family-run Brockwell Park Café (020 8671 5217) – stands in all its restored glory.

Originally built between 1811 and 1813, it was at one time a late Georgian centrepiece of the Brockwell estate of John Blades – a well-off City glass maker. It survived fire in 1990 and 2001 and after reconstruction now presents a combination of 'free Grecian' and Victorian splendour. Fronted by cedars and oak trees on the south side, a cast iron veranda sits to the left of the main stone-pillared entrance. At the weekend just follow the appetising smell of early morning fry-ups and you are sure to find the busy café. On the north side of the hall, the black Tritton clocktower is permanently stuck at 10.45 and straddles a series of paths that offer terrific vistas of London's landscape. From here you can see Battersea Power Station to the north, the London Eye and Houses of Parliament to the west, while to the east the BT Tower, Norman Foster's 'gherkin' and the winking tip of Canary Wharf are laid out in the distance. Not bad for a vantage point that's a ten-minute walk from Brixton.

Did you know?

In 1992, the Effra Redevelopment Agency launched a campaign to bring back the part of the Effra River that once flowed along the edge of Brockwell Park.

Burgess Park

Area: Approx 170 acres
Albany Road, SE5
Tel: 020 7525 1050
Transport: Elephant & Castle LU/Rail; Bus 12, 42, 63, 68, 171, 343
Open: Daily 24 hours
Facilities: Playground, cricket pitch, tennis courts, football pitch, fishing

Burgess Park sprang up in 1943 to give South Londoners a bit more natural open space. This meant levelling streets and rows of houses, with the understandably disgruntled residents being packed off to occupy the nearby Aylesbury Estate. The park runs from Camberwell to the Old Kent Road, and in the 19th century, much of it was industrial. Remnants of those commercial days are discernable in landmarks like the old lime kiln.

Like two parks in one, the Camberwell end of Burgess Park is basically a stretch of flat green land, not over dominated by trees, but with areas of meadow that give it some character. Ideal for Frisbees, kite-flying and five-a-side football, it can seem slightly overshadowed by the surrounding buildings. However, it's popular in the summer with Latin festivals and local youth carnivals being held here.

On the northern edge towards the park's centre, Chumleigh Gardens is a throwback to the 19th century, with its listed and neatly-kept almshouses near Albany Road. Rows of cottage-style garden plots growing plants from Asia, the Caribbean and the English countryside are to be found here. Dubbed Chumleigh Village, this area also offers family and schools projects which are organised by Art in the Park (0207 277 4297). Further on, at the Old Kent Road end, a huge duck pond near the far corner has open edges that are ideal for feeding and bonding with the wildfowl. Stern signs warn against swimming or fishing, although part of the lake is stocked for anglers who can buy Thames Water day or annual fishing licences. Hilly mounds, tree-lined paths, picnic areas and modest woodlands make this the far more serene end of the park.

Crystal Palace Park

Area: Approx 200 acres
Thicket Road, SE20
Tel: 020 8778 9496
Transport: Crystal Palace Rail
Open: Daily dawn til dusk
Facilities: Cricket pitch, National Sports Centre, fishing lake
Café

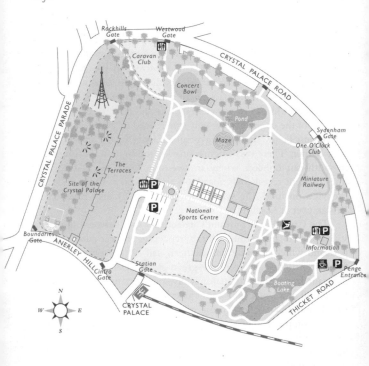

The 200 acres of Crystal Palace park are steeped in 19th and early 20th-century history. It's no surprise that there's constant disagreement between different interests as to how to recapture its former glory. The park began with the world famous Crystal Palace glass hall. Designed by Joseph Paxton, it was originally constructed for the 1851 Great Exhibition in Hyde Park. Three years later it was moved to Sydenham Hill and opened by Queen Victoria. Three times the length of St Paul's Cathedral, it housed everything connected with British industry, empire and culture, from kitchen utensils and machinery to ancient Egyptian and Renaissance art and architecture. A fire devastated the venue in 1936, but remnants of its Victorian splendour are marked by the bust of Joseph Paxton at the entrance to the National Sports Centre, and the ruins of the grand Italian terraces that run along the main avenue from the Anerley Hill entrance. Back in the Palace's heyday, the terraces' steps and plinths had statues representing the national dress of each country of the empire. Now only one fenced off figure survives on a level just below the two Egyptian sphinxes in the upper north-west corner. These two enigmas provide the highest viewing point in south-east London, where an awesome panorama of the green hues of Kent reveals hills, meadows and industry. On a good day the view includes the white towers of the Queen Elizabeth II Bridge over at Dartford.

The Crystal Palace grounds are actually split between the 1970s style concrete areas around the sports centre and car parks, and the parkland which takes up the southern half of the complex. Some recent restructuring within the green areas means that the famous dinosaur lake – with its anatomically incorrect models – has been fenced off and landscaped to include better rock formations, tidier islands and a better flow to the tidal lake that sits beside it. While this is an improvement, regular users complain that children can no longer sit in the mouths of the fourteen beasts. The restrictions are, however, inevitable given that these original figures have recently been granted listed building status.

Another park landmark is the concert bowl, a concrete structure surrounded by a lily pond which is best seen at night when the floodlights are on. It's the site of summer music festivals with local musicians, and children's events on the surrounding lawns, but has in the past hosted big name visitors such as The Cure, Bob Marley and John Lee Hooker. Just behind the moated bowl, a gravel path is the last remnant of a former motor racing track that was originally built in 1928. It is now surrounded by the flat beds of an English landscaped garden that leads to the entrance of a circular maze reconstructed in its original Victorian style, and planted with rhododendron bushes, hornbeams and poplars. Beyond this, the members only fishing lake sits at the edge of a hilly woodland area that swoops down along a path leading to the wide and open cricket field. At the far end of the lawn, the children's play area and information centre building sit just beside a glorious path of elegantly arching London planes.

Did you know?

FA Cup Finals took place at Crystal Palace from 1894 to 1924.

The Crystal Palace fire happened on the night of 30 November 1936. It took 90 fire engines to put out the flames, which could be seen from as far away as Brighton.

Known for its old dinosaurs, Crystal Palace was the venue for The Sex Pistols last 'Jubilee' gig in July 2002.

Crystal Palace Park

Dulwich Park

Area: Approx 72 acres
College Road, SE21
Tel: 020 8693 5737
Transport: North Dulwich and West Dulwich Rail
Open: Daily 8am-dusk
Facilities: Children's playground, cricket pitch, tennis court, bowling green, boating lake
Café

The seventy-two acres of Dulwich Park were once used as farmland (known as Five Fields) before being landscaped for the public in 1890. Ancient oaks were used as boundary markers, and many of them still stand within the park today. Sandy paths beyond the sports pitches are used by horse-riders from the Dulwich Riding School (tel 020 8693 2944), and for the non-horsey there are funky bikes for hire from London Recumbents (tel 020 8299 6636 / *www.londonrecumbents.com)* with lessons on tandems, trikes and horizontal bikes all bookable from the Ranger's Yard. The park is situated near three schools, making its open lawns a popular place for organised sports sessions on the football and cricket pitches.

Of the four entrances, the main College Road gate faces the John Soane-designed Dulwich Picture Gallery, said to be the oldest purpose-built arthouse in London. Central to the park is the lake, where boats can be hired all year round (weekends only during the winter). On the lake's south side, a 1970s Barbara Hepworth 'Two Forms' sculpture stands on a grassy knoll, while over towards the north side, the white wood and glass-fronted Pavilion Restaurant and café serves full meals, and is especially busy on weekend mornings. At the back of the building is the pretty Dry Garden, where aromatic plants like lavender and other herbs offer up their scent. This isn't the only garden within the park. A few others are scattered throughout, but the American Garden, with a healthy selection of rhododendrons and azaleas stands out. Best appreciated in the summer for its colourful blooms, it also has a number of large silver birches that shade the flowers when the sun is out. The paths away from the lake lead towards the playground, through the trees you can spot the top of the steel-built Crystal Palace Tower.

Other green areas beyond Dulwich Park are Sydenham Hill Woods towards Crystal Palace Park. Owned by the London Wildlife Trust it has a ruined monastery, and is one of the largest remnants of the Great North Wood. Even closer to Dulwich Park is the beautifully refurbished Belair Park. The only Grade II listed landscape in the borough, it has a central lake, park lodge, stable building and pitches for cricket and football.

Belair Park
Gallery Road and Thurlow Park Road, SE21
Tel: 020 8525 1050
Transport: West Dulwich Rail; Bus P4

Sydenham Hill Woods
Sydenham Hill and Crescent Wood Road, SE26
Tel: 020 8699 5698
Transport: Forest Hill Rail; Bus 63

Map labels

N W E S (compass)

DLR
CUTTY SARK

GREENWICH

KING WILLIAM WLK

ROMNEY RD

PARK ROW

TRAFALGAR RD

National Maritime Museum

Queen's House

PARK VISTA

MAZE HILL

St Mary's Gate

Herb Garden

The Avenue

Boating Lake

One Tree Hill

Lover's Walk

MAZE HILL

Maze Hill Gate

Royal Observatory

Tumuli

Queen Elizabeth's Oak

Roman Ruin

Crooms Hill Gate

Macartney House

Reservoir

Blackheath Avenue

Great Cross Avenue

The Gardens

Tennis

Woodland Walk

CHESTERFIELD WALK

Ranger's House

Bower Avenue

Ranger's Field

Lake

The Wilderness (Deer Park)

Park office

Blackheath Gate

CHARLTON WAY

Greenwich Park

Area: Approx 183 acres
Blackheath Gate, Charlton Way, SE10
Tel: 020 8293 0703/858 9695
Open: Daily 6am-dusk
Transport: Cutty Sark DLR, Greenwich DLR/Rail, Maze Hill Rail;
Bus 1, 53, 177, 180, 188, 286; riverboat to Greenwich Pier
Facilities: Children's playground and boating pool, tennis courts, put-
ting green, cricket pitch, rugby pitch
Cafés

The site of the start of the annual London Marathon, Greenwich Park is the only royal green space east of Central London. Lying between Blackheath and the Thames, it is just a few miles to the south of the planned Olympic zone in the Lower Lea Valley.

Having stood in its 183 acres of grounds since 1433, the park has been lavished with care and attention due to its titled connections and maritime history. This riverside location was once the site of the Palace of Placentia, the birthplace of Henry VIII and his daughters Mary and Elizabeth. It was a favourite royal residence enclosed with 200 acres of pasture, wood and heath in an area that now makes up the current royal park.

Undeniably magnificent, Greenwich Park offers huge expanses of flat and spectacularly hilly green areas, that are cut through with grand avenues and smaller paths. There are many other noteworthy historic buildings in the area including the former Royal Naval College (now the University of Greenwich), The Old Royal Observatory and Planetarium, The Fan Museum, The Queen's House (see page 149) and The Ranger's House.

If you enter the park from the Maritime Museum entrance, you might want to fuel up at the white-washed St Mary's Lodge Café. Doubling up as a snack spot and information centre, it offers cakes, hot drinks and sandwiches, as well as leaflets and a potted history of the park in the attached information centre. A huge 'tidying up' programme takes place during autumn and winter, when thousands of daffodil and crocus bulbs are planted, alongside equally large numbers of plants like pansies and wallflowers. The well-kept borders and seasonal changes are all achieved by state of the art computer technology, which determines the planting schedule and the number of plants required.

For the best views, the park's highest point is at the Royal Observatory where the imposing monument of General James Wolfe stands. It is here that the tree-lined Blackheath Avenue meets Great Cross Avenue. At around fifty metres above sea level, you can look down onto the Thames, and take in the panoramic view of St Paul's Cathedral, Tower Bridge (on a good day) and Canary Wharf. The main art deco Pavilion café is also found at the park's summit, while a short walk from here is the fallen Queen Elizabeth Oak. A natural monument to bygone times, it is said to have been planted in the 12th century. Storms tipped over the long dead husk in 1991, and it's now preserved within a metal-gated enclosure. Linked with Queen Elizabeth I, who used its six foot hollow trunk as a resting spot, and Henry VIII and Anne Boleyn who danced round it – at one time it also had a door added as a lock up for criminals. It now has a new fledgling oak by its side, which was planted by the Duke of Edinburgh in 1992.

The areas towards Blackheath are the lushest parts of the park. The flower garden beside the enclosed deer park offers some glorious bursts of colour during the summer, while the cedars have branches low enough to provide some privacy for those wanting to relax in the shade. Sturdy clusters of thick oaks and birches make this area seem like a park within a park, especially with the central lake, fountain and wildfowl. There's a stunted look to some of the trees here, a consequence of their branches having been cut during the Second World War to widen the firing range for anti-aircraft guns. Greenwich has a smattering of signs saying where you can't cycle, play sports or unleash your dogs but seems a lot more relaxed than other royal parks like Hyde Park or St James's Park. There are more than enough sports areas to compensate for the restrictions.

Greenwich Park

Close to Blackheath Gate on the park's south side, the Rangers' Field is marked out for cricket, where teams can hire the pitch and pavilion. At the edge of the field, the Dell is a lovely enclosed rhododendron and azalea garden, surrounded by a path that leads on to the lively rose garden not far from the putting green. Rangers House (020 8853 0035) is located here and is one of the park's gems, containing a very fine art collection which is well worth a visit when the weather is bad. Nearby, the Greenwich Park Tennis Centre has six hard courts, which open from April to September (phone 0208 293 0276 for times), and an adjacent putting green with equipment for hire. Summer and school holidays bring puppet shows and workshops for children, with Sunday concerts in the bandstand.

Did you know?

Members of the public have been enjoying the Park since the early 1700s when passes were issued to local people. In 1830 the park was opened to all.

The tumuli are a series of saucer-shaped mounds inside Greenwich Park. Many of them were destroyed by planting, but in 1784, when several of them were opened, human hair, scraps of woollen cloth and glass beads were discovered.

The second wedding in Four Weddings and A Funeral was filmed in the chapel in the Old Royal Naval College.

On the opposite side of the park, Vanbrugh Castle at 121 Maze Hill was used in the 1986 film Mona Lisa, and close to the entrance of Greenwich Park, the Gloucester Pub was featured in the 1996 film Beautiful Thing.

Greenwich Park was one of the locations used for the 1995 film Sense and Sensibility starring Emma Thompson.

Greenwich Peninsular Ecology Park

Area: Approx 4 acres
Thames Path, John Harrison Way, SE10
Transport: North Greenwich LU; Bus 108, 161, 188, 422, 472, 486
Tel: 020 8293 1904
Open: Wed-Sun 10am-5pm

Along the Thames Path, and behind the up-and-coming Millennium Village with its marketing suites, new-build apartments and shops, is this wonderfully ecology park. A marshy oasis for visiting and resident wildfowl, it's an area made up of two lakes surrounded by woodland. There's free public access to the outer lake at any time, but the inner lake can only be reached through the gatehouse and information centre during opening hours. Mondays and Tuesdays are reserved for school visits during term time, when children can take part in quizzes, nature trails, pond dipping and bird spotting.

At one time this was agricultural land, which was industrialised from the late 1880s. With the closure of the gasworks in the 1970s, the land slowly fell into dereliction. The four-acre park was finally created by English Partnerships in 1997, and is now run by the Trust for Urban Ecology.

There are in fact eight main habitats in the park – lakes, marsh, shingle, beach, shallow pools, wildflower meadow, willow beds and woodland. Together they form a thriving area of wildlife. During a walk around both lakes visitors can see butterflies, dragon or damselflies and stag beetles as well as newts, frogs and voles in their favoured habitats. The riverbank is an ideal spot for watching the varied birds that visit the park throughout the year. The specially designed hides allow keen spotters to observe the seasonal changes in feathered traffic, from gulls, geese and moorhens to ducks, reed warblers and kingfishers. Like Thames Barrier Park, this green space is often quiet, offering visitors the chance to bond with nature or simply escape from the bustle of the city.

Horniman Gardens

Approx 16 acres
100 London Road, Forest Hill, London, SE23
Tel: 020 8699 1872
Transport: Forest Hill Rail; Bus 185, 176, P4
Open: Daily dawn til dusk
Facilities: Animal/bird enclosure
Café

Forest Hill's best known landmark has to be the Horniman
Museum with its gallery collections of natural history, world cul-
tures and musical instruments. The museum collection is well
worth a visit, but so are the museum's surrounding acres of gorgeous
gardens. Beautifully maintained since the museum opened in 1901,
there are formal and natural landscapes and expansive north facing
views from where you can look across the valley to distant north
London. Within the grounds, the fine rose garden and sunken
Italian gardens are ideal for a peacefully stroll. The central bandstand that dates back to 1912 is also worth a visit. Other features
include a Grade II listed conservatory by the Museum's café, a five
acre nature trail and an animal enclosure with goats, rabbits and
turkeys. The conservatory gets occasional use for functions and
concerts, but during the summer, the gardens' lawns are also well-
used for music festivals, visiting bands or children's days. The
Horniman Gardens with its extensive grounds, museum and animal
enclosure make it a great place for a family day out.

Myatt's Fields

Area: Approx 10.4 acres
Cormont Road, SE5
Tel: 020 7926 6200
Transport: Loughborough Rail; Bus P5
Open: Daily dawn til dusk
Facilities: Children's play area, tennis courts, football pitch
and putting green

A modestly-sized Victorian space in a quiet corner of Camberwell, Myatt's Fields has a pristine character all of its own. Surrounded by neat residential red-brick houses, it's a park that is popular with the locals. The name derives from Joseph Myatt, an early Victorian farmer, much respected for his skills in growing strawberries. Myatt largely made his fortune through commercially growing rhubarb, then a luxury food in the UK.

The park's features include a bandstand (often used by children as a climbing frame), an ornamental garden, clusters of well tended flowerbeds, well tendered lawns and an enclosed picnic area. This latter facility is of a fair size, but there are only three tables and as many benches for visitors to fight over in the summer. The adjacent children's play area is large, with swings, slides, frames and a paddling pool. Within the rest of the park, dog areas are conscientiously used by owners anxious to avoid the punishing £1000 fine for any canine misdeeds. Dusk is a lovely time to visit, particularly during the summer and even late autumn when early evening joggers start lapping the park's oval edges. The couples hanging out in the garden seem content to soak up the relative quiet only sporadically broken by cheers from the football pitch.

Peckham Rye Park

Area: Approx 49 acres
Peckham Rye, Homestall Road,
Colyton Road, Strakers Road, SE15/SE22
Tel: 020 8693 3791
Transport: Peckham Rye Rail; Bus 12, 37, 63, 78, 312, 484, P12
Open: Summer 10am-5pm; winter 10am-3.30pm
Facilities: Bowling green and pavilion, football pitches

Peckham Rye Park was once the site of the late 19th-century Homestall Farm. It lies on the northern boundary of the larger Peckham Rye Common towards Forest Hill and the leafy Honour Oak. Although the park's flat outer edges are mainly open fields split by paths and interspersed with a few old wooden climbing frames, it does have the added appeal of the Peck River. The river runs along the east side of the park and flows underground into the park's pond and the stream inside the central Japanese Garden.

The Japanese Garden is situated within the park's woodland-surrounded middle section. After a long refurbishment that started in winter 2003, this section of the park was reopened in June 2005. It contains an American Garden, the Sexby English Garden, flowered arbours and Visitor Centre all restored to their original 19th-century glory. Contemporary additions to the park are the wildlife and conservation area.

Ruskin Park

Area: Approx 32 acres
Denmark Hill, Camberwell, SE5
Tel: 0207 733 6659
Transport: Loughborough Rail; Bus 40, 42, 68, 176, 185, 468
Facilities: Playground, paddling pool, netball court, tennis court

In the heat of the summer, the large shallow paddling pool at the north-west corner of the park is alive with the yelps of delight from hordes of children splashing around to their hearts' content. A small picnic area and adjacent playground make this the most happening spot during summer holidays.

The rest of the park also has some fine features. A wide meadow area is circled by a path that's a jogger's delight, while the northern end has a large duck pond and a flower garden with a bricked and arboured walkway with overhanging plants, dramatically tangled branches and rhododendron bushes. The enclosed area next door with its raised lawn, hedges and shaded benches for summer readers can get spectacularly overgrown during autumn and winter, but the outer surrounding lawns and bright pockets of flowerbeds are always immaculately kept, and serve as a favoured spot for sunbathers. They have also become a regular location for many a wedding photocall over the years.

Never overcrowded, Ruskin Park is perfect for sitting and doing absolutely nothing, and watching the huge population of squirrels who are so laid back they'll practically eat out of your hands.

Sunray Gardens

Area: Approx 4 acres
Red Post Hill, SE24
Tel: 0207 525 0874
Transport: North Dulwich Rail
Open: Summer 8am-9pm, winter 8am-4.30pm
Facilities: Playground, basketball court

This small neighbourhood park at the bottom of a hill was once the water garden of the 'Casina' villa, which was built for lawyer Richard Shaw in 1796. The grounds originally covered 15 acres, with the estates and houses that now surround the present day park once being a series of gardens and small fields leading down a slope to the current park and pond.

The park got its current name in 1923, and while its boundaries follow that of the original Casina villa many new features have been added. The gardens now include a colourful children's playground with a wooden ship being the most popular piece of climbing equipment, a picnic area with rock features that work well as extra seating, small flowerbeds, paved walkways, and at the far southern end, a large duck pond with a feeding platform. Labelled trees circle the pond, with a weeping ash, a Chinese Ginko biloba and a dramatically leaning horse chestnut taking pride of place.

Sydenham Wells

Area: Approx 19 acres
Wells Park Road, Sydenham SE26
Transport: Rail
Open: 8am till dusk
Facilities: Playground, water-play system, tennis courts, ponds
Refreshment kiosk

Close to Crystal Palace, the smaller but equally well-loved Sydenham Wells Park sits in an area that was once part of a landscape of sweeping hills, streams and valleys that occupied over 500 acres of what is now urban south east London. Today, the relatively compact park has a series of contemporary features including two tennis courts, a multi-sports ball court, a summer putting green, ponds and a large children's playground. The park achieved Green Flag status in 2004, no doubt for its beautifully landscaped gardens boasting a banquet of shrubs, trees and seasonal bedding. The state-of-the-art water-play fun facility has also gone some way in helping take Sydenham Wells Park out of the shadow of the better-known Crystal Palace park and is packed with scores of children and families during the hot summer months.

Water has always featured highly in Sydenham Wells Park, with its name coming from the medicinal springs, which were discovered in Sydenham in the mid-17th century. For a while, these were a popular attraction for the village, turning it into a spa resort, until the novelty of drinking the bitter-tasting valley water wore off in the early 19th century. A number of the 12 original wells still lie within the park's grounds and the water-play area is sourced by the springs. Officially opened to the public in 1901, this park continues to be one of the gems of south-east London.

Tibetan Peace Garden

Area: Approx 16 acres
Geraldine Mary Harmsworth Park
(next to Imperial War Museum), St George's Road, SE1
Tel: 020 7525 0874
Transport: Elephant and Castle LU/Rail, Lambeth North LU;
Bus 171, 176, 188, 344, C10
Open: Daily 8am-9pm (summer) and 8am-4.30pm (winter)
Facilities: basketball court

The grounds that surround the Imperial War Museum have had a bit of a rough ride in the past. They are often used as a functional walk-through area for those with a particular interest in the museum's wares despite the attractions of a children's play area and basketball court. The situation improved in 1999 when Trudy Styler (Sting's wife) and the Dalai Lama ceremoniously opened the Tibetan Peace Garden, located within the main Geraldine Mary Harmsworth Park.

Created to establish a place of peace and harmony, it seems fitting that the garden lies in front of the museum building, which was once the site of the famous 19th-century Bedlam asylum. The entrance has a stone Language Pillar, each side carved with a message of peace from the Dalai Lama in Tibetan, English, Chinese and Hindi. Three carved steps at the top of the pillar represent peace, understanding and love. The garden's central focus is a bronze mandala, with eight meditation seats. More westernised sculptures are laid out to the north, south, east and west corners of the garden, with these areas representing the four elements of air, fire, earth and water.

Scattered throughout are herbs and plants from Tibet and the Himalayas. Climbing plants like honeysuckle, jasmine and scented roses all add to the sense of tranquillity. The landscape of trees that surrounds the whole area ensures that this site – which is a haven for those in or out of tune with Buddhist philosophies – is worthy of its official title of Samten Kyil, (Garden of Contemplation).

Tibetan Peace Garden

East London

Haggerston Park

Area: Approx 14.6 acres
Queensbridge Road, E2
Tel: 020 7739 6288
Transport: Bus 26, 48, 55
Open: Summer Mon-Sun 7am-10pm; winter 7am-5pm
Facilities: Football pitch, BMX cycle track

Home to the perennially popular Hackney City Farm, Haggerston Park opens out into a nature reserve, which consists of a section of meadowland, with banks of shrubs and tall grasses in view of a fenced and turfed football pitch and children's play area. Signs warning against swimming or paddling in the nearby pond seem needless unless there are locals with the urge to soak in dark soupy water amongst overgrown weeds and discarded shopping bags. These are the usual sign of the end of the summer, but it's fair to say that despite some regeneration, Haggerston Park feels rather neglected compared to the more popular urban farm site. However, the banks of hilly wooded areas behind the farm offer a good retreat from the Hackney traffic. Across the Hackney Road entrance to the farm and the park, there's Ion Square Gardens, another modest area of E8 green, with a children's area at the far end and an open field for occasional music festivals and other events.

London Fields

Area: 30 acres
Lansdowne Drive, Hackney, E8
Transport: London Fields Rail
Open: Daily 24 hours
Facilities: Lido, children's playgrounds, tennis courts, table tennis,
bmx track and cricket pitch

London Fields is first mentioned in 1540 as common land used by farmers to graze cattle before sending them to market. In the last two hundred years Hackney has been swallowed up in London's expansion and London Fields has become an oasis of green amid the urban sprawl. Martin Amis used the area as the title for his novel of the late 1980s, but the book's dystopia of cheap larger, dodgy geezers and semi-pro darts is a long way from the increasingly gentrified area today. The nearby Broadway Market is now a very popular food market on Saturdays which attracts an increasingly wealthy local population.

The park itself is a pleasant, if rather flat, 30 acre green space complete with tennis courts, several playgrounds, an outdoor table tennis table and a small BMX track. The cricket strip hosts competitive matches throughout the summer and is the home of London Fields CC. There are further improvements planned for London Fields with the re-opening of the Lido in the summer of 2006, after over fifteen years of closure and dereliction. The Lido will have a retractable roof allowing it to open throughout the year and will be one of the few 50 metre pools in London. Visitors looking for relaxation rather than sporting activity will find plenty of shade from the many mature trees in London Fields. The park has no café, but there is The Pub on the Park to the eastern side, which has a balcony overlooking London Fields.

Mile End Park

Area: Approx 22 acres
Mile End Road, E3
Tel: 020.8525 4337
Transport: Mile End LU
Open: Daily 24 hours
Facilities: Play area, Ecology park, Artspark, climbing wall, sports park,
go-karts

An East End treasure, Mile End Park stretches from Limehouse along the Regent's Canal and over towards its larger sibling Victoria Park. The unenclosed acres were made available to the public in 1945, and underwent vast refurbishment in 2002 with the help of £25 million of funding. The development involved the creation of separate parks including the Artspark, Ecology Park and Terrace Garden all near Mile End Road, which cuts through the middle of the park.

Mile End Park

Following a campaign by residence the local council built the Green Bridge which provides a grassy, tree-lined walkway and cycle path that crosses over the main road and gives the park some continuity as well as providing great views of Canary Wharf in the distance.

Mile End Park is an elongated strip of green land, with the terraced garden being its prettiest spot. This is found at the edge of the Green Bridge, and is shielded from Mile End Road by a thick row of trees. It's a quiet area with colourful plants and seating arranged around a central pond and cascading fountain. Over towards the north, beyond the bridge, the Ecology Park also has a secluded lake, and a wind turbine used to power a pump that circulates water to the park's three lakes. The Ecology Centre building is a venue for park ranger training in everything from horticulture to graffiti removal, as well as hosting nature events for the public.

The Artspark should see the addition of a park pavilion, as well as an 'art mound' (exhibition space), and eventually a Henry Moore sculpture, which was benevolently left to the East End by the artist. There are intermittent art events in the park though, as well as workshops in park design for children.

Down at the southern end of the park, there's a change of focus in the facilities. An open space for ball games, circus events, funfairs and festivals. Nearby is The Ragged School Museum and a children's playground with climbing frame and rope slide. Further along there's the go-kart area and sports stadium, featuring an eight-lane athletics track, grass and artificial football pitches, a weight training room, changing facilities and swimming pool. Plans for further development include a swimming pool and other outdoor sports areas. An established attraction is the Mile End Climbing Wall (020 8980 0289), a few minutes from Mile End tube station at Haverfield Road. The place is run by climbing enthusiasts in a converted pipe-bending factory and is always busy. Classes are available for children and adults of all standards.

Springfield Park

Area: Approx 32 acres
Springfield Lane, E4
Tel: 020 7923 3660
Open: Summer 7.30am-9pm, winter 7.30am-dusk
Transport: Clapton Rail; Bus 253
Facilities: Children's playground, tennis courts, bowling green
Café

Opened in 1905, Springfield Park overlooks the River Lea and the expanse of the Walthamstow Marshes. Spanning the steep grounds of what used to be three private houses, only the park's Springfield House (now the White Lodge Café) survives. The café is open throughout the summer, but only at weekends in the winter when things are quieter. The building has dramatic French windows that open out onto the garden, and a drawing room serving hot and cold meals and exhibiting work by local artists. From the east side of the lodge, the duck pond widens out from the bottom of a sloping path. You can step right down to the edge, where the wildfowl pick at reeds in water that also holds Japanese koi carp.

The old glasshouses on the other side of the café have now become a tropical conservatory, with green-fingered activity by the volunteer group, *Growing Communities*, who host Open Sunday sessions every third weekend. Salad crops, basil and oakleaf lettuce are some of the spoils, as well as oyster mushrooms in a composting area. Figs, olives and grapes are work in progress in one of the greenhouses. Elsewhere, pockets of dense (but safe) woodland make excellent hide and seek areas for energetic children, while mature trees (including copper beech, plane, sweet chestnut, silver birch, lime and mulberry) stake out their territory among the lawns. Although the park's bowling green is slightly shabby, with jumbled hedgerows and rosebushes framing a pretty decrepit pavilion, other features compensate for the shortfall. The benches cloaked by neat hedges along the curving path at the brow of the hill are a great spot to sit and admire the view.

Down the park's slope lie the tennis courts, children's playground and allotment area and beyond this is the Springfield Marina where a colourful hotchpotch of boats are docked. Cross over the white bridge to the Lee Valley which contains all the ditches, ponds and shrublands of the Walthamstow Nature Reserve. The park's connection to the Lee Valley network of canals and waterways is one of its great advantages. From here you can walk or cycle South to Hackney Marshes or further on to Victoria Park (see page 105) or head north to Walthamstow Marshes or even further on to Waltham Abbey.

Thames Barrier Park

Area: Approx 22 acres
Barrier Point Road, off North Woolwich Road, E16
Tel: 020 7511 4111
Open: Daily dawn til dusk
Transport: Canning Town LU/DLR then 474 bus, Stratford LU;
Bus 69
Facilities: Children's playground, basketball court
Café

Completed in 2001, Thames Barrier Park is London's first entirely new green space in recent history – around fifty years in fact. Formerly an undeveloped river bank, it sits on the north side of the River Thames at Silvertown. Overlooking the huge metal fins of the Thames Barrier floodworks, the park is a quirky area offering a range of natural features and playing fields close to smart riverside apartments and a flat industrial landscape.

The park is a perfect haven for high and low tide wildlife that are attracted to the shore. From the Pavilion of Remembrance (which honours the victims of the Blitz) visitors can see herons, teal, shelduck and mallards. The wildflower meadow with its population of crickets creates a cacophony during the summer, and a fountain plaza – with blasts of rising water jets – is also a summertime treat for excitable children (and adults). There's a children's play area and small unfenced basketball court, which looks like a bit of an after-thought, with a rickety ballpost at one end and a miniature football net at the other.

The Green Dock Garden is a sunken rectangular row of hedges, flowerbeds and paths, which is cut into a scooped area between the riverfront and the fountain area. If viewed from the overhead walkways, this strip of greenery actually looks like it has been set within the remnants of a concrete strip of motorway, although it is actually a very lush area with banks of hedges and neatly cut flower beds.

The whole park can be comfortably viewed from the visitors pavilion – the central glass-fronted building with oakwood frame and iroko decking. This is the home of the Prima Coffee café, offering bagels, croissants and freshly ground coffee. There's a temporary car park near the entrance, and the new DLR station should make this a more accessible park for those using public transport.

Thames Barrier Park

Victoria Park

Area: Approx 218 acres
Old Ford Road, E3
Tel: 020 8533 2057
Open: Daily 6am-dusk; closed 25 Dec
Transport: Mile End LU, Cambridge Heath or Hackney Wick Rail;
Bus 8, 26, 30, 55
Facilities: Tennis courts, bowling green, fishing (with free licence),
children's playground, Victoria Park Harriers and Tower Hamlets
Athletics Club
Café

It took five years to create this park, which eventually opened its
gates to the public in 1845. It's opening followed a petition from
over 30,000 local residents to Queen Victoria for some decent outdoor space. Victoria Park also contains what was once called
Bonners Field, where during the time of Bishop Bonner heretics
were publicly burned. Soon after its optimistic opening it was the
scene of the Chartist Riots of 1848, undermining its claim to be the
Regent's Park of the East End.

Today, the sprawling acres, which cover parts of Bethnal Green,
Hackney and Bow host regular festivals, fêtes, sports rallies and meet-
ings, and although not as pristine as some of London's real royal
parks, the neat Victorian lampposts and wrought iron gates give this
open space its own noble character. The park is bounded by the
Regent's Canal to the west, which is joined by the Hertford Canal
along the southern edge, and boasts a staggering number of trees
(over 4,500 throughout), many of which are as old as the park itself.
Three special walks designed by Tower Hamlets (020 7985 1957)
allow full appreciation of these fine specimens, with the areas to the
east, west and along the park's outer avenues planted with species of
sycamores, maples, false acacias, Kentucky coffee trees, London
planes and limes.

Often considered as three parks in one, due to divisions by
major avenues, Victoria Park is actually cleanly cut through by

Grove Road on the west side between the Royal Gates and Crown Gates. The larger end of the park to the east is more open, with tennis courts, the old lake and duck pond, fallow deer enclosure and bandstand being some of the features surrounded by wide and open areas of mainly flat lawns and grassland often populated by local schools playing football. The park is also the training ground for the Victoria Park Harriers and Tower Hamlets Athletics Club, (020 7249 2590) whose club house is a former church hall at the junction of Cadogan Terrace and Victoria Park Road at the eastern edge of the park.

On a historical note, the entrance to the west side of the park has the famous statues of the crazy-looking Grecian Dogs of Alcibiades. Donated to Victoria Park in 1912, over the years they've gone through cleaning, restoration and vandalism. They are now in a shameful state sporting smashed faces and broken legs but still soldier on as battered reminders of the parks former grandeur. Just a minutes walk from the dogs is the huge lake within the park's grounds with its powerful fountain and a good number of ducks, geese and other wild fowl. The country's oldest model moat club meets here every second Sunday of the month and there's fishing for all with a free licence. This is also the site of the refurbished Pavilion Café which serves hot and cold drinks and snacks. From here the canal towpath that runs along the parks border will take you east to Mile End Park (see page 99) or west towards Islington.

Did you know?

When Victoria Park was opened in 1845, around 700 fruit trees – which were thought to encourage 'disorder' were removed and replaced by evergreens.

Victoria Park

West Ham Park

Area: Approx 77 acres
Upton Lane, London E7
Tel: 020 8472 3584
Transport: Stratford LU/Rail
Open: Daily 7.30am-dusk
Facilities: Children's playground, tennis courts, football pitches, cricket pitches, all weather pitch, summer running track, rounders area, Essex Cricket Club sports clinic
Refreshment kiosk

A Corporation of London treasure, West Ham Park takes its reputation for providing excellent public sporting facilities just as seriously as that of its five times Green Flag-winning status. With nine tennis courts, two cricket squares, two football pitches, a large rounders area and running track, it's no wonder that this is the borough's most popular site for local schools' sports days, or that regular training for the 2008 Beijing Olympics takes place here. Annual tennis clinics run through the spring and summer, as well as a cricket clinic for under-16s run by the Essex Cricket Club (phone for details).

Opened to the public in 1874, the park is thought to date back to the 16th century. Naturally flat, there are a few man-made hills giving the vast green areas surrounding the sports facilities a tad more character, as well as providing spots to picnic on or hide behind. A loyal stream of up to a million visitors a year passes through the park, many heading straight for the exquisite enclosed ornamental garden at the far south-eastern edge. An alpine rockery forms the centre of this area, with paths separating the surrounding sections of rhododendron and heather beds, the terrace and footbridge, as well as the three separate walled, iris and rose gardens. The latter is filled with up to 70 different rose types, including the City of London, Just Joey and Sexy Rexy – all award winners in their own right.

Behind the first cricket pitch towards the south-east of the main park, the nursery, with its huge computer-controlled greenhouses, provides thousands of plants for the entire City of London. The park's floral displays are replenished by activities like the recent community bulb planting project, when hundreds of local school children rolled up their sleeves to help plant 9,000 daffodil bulbs. In terms of the park's trees, the sweet gum is one of the newer species, joining cedars, weeping ash, hornbeam and oak. Summer sees an appealing choice of activities for children including puppet shows and magicians on the bandstand, or live music events. A full-time attendant is on hand in The Wendy Corner – the children's playground – which also has a pre-war paddling pool (open daily 1 June-7 Sept).

Outer London

Bushy Park

Area: Approx 1100 acres
Hampton Court Road, Hampton Hill, TW12
Tel: 020 8979 1586
Transport: Hampton Court, Kingston or Teddington Rail
Open: Summer 5am-10.30pm, winter 5am-7pm
Facilities: Football pitches, cricket and rugby pitches, hockey pitches,
tennis courts, open air pool (heated), gym, fishing ponds

Of the extensive royal parks in or around London, Bushy Park is perhaps less known (or less written about) than its siblings. Its flat landscape is second in size to the mammoth Richmond Park, but still retains its own regal character. Lying to the north of Hampton Court Palace, it has some historical links with the building, which in the 17th century suffered from a chronic lack of water. It was Charles I who came up with the idea of having an artificial river in the park as a much needed reservoir for water to supply the parched royal household. It took nine months to build the 'false' Longford River, which still exists today, and at thirteen miles long, runs from its source at Longford Point on the River Colne, beyond Heathrow Airport. A linear nature reserve stretches for around nine miles outside the park's boundaries, with grass banks, shrubs and trees along the length of the river.

There's plenty of water within the park itself with streams and ponds attracting swans, coots and other wildfowl. There are also lakes for fishing and facilities for horse riding. Bushy park also has herds of red and fallow deer within its grounds.

The park's most formal area is the central Chestnut Walk, a beautiful mile-long avenue between huge chestnut trees, which runs between Hampton Court Road in Hampton and Sandy Lane in Teddington. Situated so far from the centre of town, Bushy Park is a long way to travel for many Londoners, but there is enough to see and do here to make it worth the effort.

Epping Forest

Area: Approx 6000 acres
Information Centre, High Beech, Loughton, Essex
Tel: 020 8508 0028
Transport: Theydon Bois LU, Loughton LU then 2-mile walk
Open: Mon-Sat 10am-5pm, Sun 11am-5pm (April-Oct); Mon-Fri
11am-3pm, Sat 10am-dusk, Sun 11am-dusk (Nov-Mar)
Facilities: Football and cricket pitches, camp sites, golf, cycle tracks,
horse riding
Café

Delightful, awesome and overwhelming are some of the adjectives that could be used to describe this 6000 acre ancient forest on the western and northern edges of Loughton, Essex. Only 15 minutes from Charing Cross by rail, it's not far from London's centre but it can be an awkward destination for unfamiliar visitors. There are car parks but if you're using public transport Theydon Bois on the Central line is the closest tube stop, although from here it's a 10-minute uphill walk to the entrance, which can be a bit of a chore, bearing in mind there'll be plenty more walking once you get to the forest. The area near to Loughton station is where you'll find the information centre, although this is a two-mile walk towards the middle section of the forest, so the best bet might be to get hold of a map★ beforehand to plan your route around the forest in advance. These might sound like fussy precautions, but at twelve miles long and two and half miles across at its widest point, this is the largest green space in Greater London, and despite the fact that the forest (which is unenclosed and uncultivated) is never more than a mile from the road, it's pretty easy to get lost among the thick woodland paths and other features that make up this huge expanse.

Managed by the Corporation of London, Epping Forest is actually much more than one big impenetrable thicket. There are a whole range of features and services including 60 football pitches, an eighteen-hole golf course, three cricket pitches and horses for hire if you want to take advantage of the numerous riding tracks throughout the forest. Two listed buildings include the restored Queen Elizabeth's Hunting Lodge on Ranger's Road in Chingford, which was originally built for Henry VIII in 1543 so he could watch the Royal Hunt. It was renovated for Queen Elizabeth in 1589 and is now used from time to time for small exhibitions open to the public. The Temple is another listed site in Wanstead Park, which lies within the forest. Dating from the late 18th century, the Temple is believed to have been built for Lord Tylney, owner of the now-demolished Wanstead House. This park also has ornamental ponds, a ruined grotto and carpets of bluebells in early spring.

From season to season the look of the forest changes dramatically, so what you get from the landscape of trees and wildlife depends on when you visit. If you can see the sun and snatches of blue skies sneaking through the top of some of the lushest tree canopies in the densest areas of the forest in the summer, that in itself is pretty eye-catching, but even in late autumn and early winter the forest has plenty to offer. Clay soil on many of the sloping paths mean things can get fairly slippery, so sturdy shoes are a must.

As one of the last surviving areas of the great oak forests that framed London until medieval times, Epping Forest is a dedicated conservation area as well as a Site of Special Scientific Interest. Whether you're a wildlife aficionado or a complete novice, expect to see hundreds of rare plants, animals and insect species with anything from dragonflies to grass snakes crossing your path.

*Maps can be ordered through the City of London website *www.cityoflondon.gov.uk* or the Epping Forest Information Centre. The Official Guide to Epping Forest (priced £1.50) is also available from the Guildhall Library Bookshop (020 7332 1858).

Did you know?

In the 18th century, the monarchy lost interest in hunting, which affected areas like Epping Forest. It became a shelter for thieves and outlaws who would frequently attack nearby villages at night.

Morden Hall Park

Area: Approx 125 acres
Morden Hall Road, Morden, SM4
Tel: 020 8545 6850
Transport: Morden LU, Morden Road Tramlink, South Merton and
Morden South Rail
Open: Daily 8am-6pm
Café, garden centre

Not far from the most southern stop on the Northern line can be found this suburban oasis of National Trust meadows, woodland and marshland. The park surrounds the large whitewashed 18th-century Morden Hall House, that's now a popular restaurant. One of its prettiest spots is the large open rose garden, with scattered rectangular flowerbeds that display a collection of over 2,000 blooms in the summer. The building beside this is the Old Snuff Mill – now an environmental study and workshop centre for everything from stained glass to wood turning. The original water wheel on the outside wall was used to grind snuff until 1922. It's from beneath its black iron spokes that a gushing section of the River Wandle travels beneath a sturdy concrete bridge, its downstream journey leading on to a decorative white cast-iron footbridge in the distance. In fact, the Wandle river meanders throughout the park, its path punctuated by features such as a rural-looking three-arch brick bridge, and a magnificent cascading weir, with large overhanging willows.

Oaks, beech, ash and birch trees are planted throughout the woodlands, with their ages spanning the 18th to the mid 20th centuries. To the north of the park, the marshland areas are popular havens for herons and kingfishers. A stable block, garden centre and riverside café are all on site, and not too far away in Merton, Deen City Farm★ has a modest number of sheep, cows, pigs and fowl, as well as a riding school.

★Deen City Farm, 39 Windsor Avenue, SW19 (020 8543 5300)

Osterley Park

Area: Approx 350 acres
Off Jersey Road, Isleworth, Middlesex, TW7
Tel: 020 8232 5050/01494 755566
Transport: Osterley LU
Open: Daily 9am-dusk
Facilities: Osterley House, Jerwood Art Gallery, farm shop

For many, the main reason for visiting Osterley Park is to snoop inside the red-bricked and white-pillared Osterley House. In 1761, the building was a crumbling Tudor pile before trendy Scottish architect Robert Adam transformed it into a lavish country villa, set in a suburban landscape. In 1949 the National Trust took over the grounds and acquired the farmland in the late 1990s. With the support of the Friends of Osterley Park, the trust has funded the growing of flowers for displays in the house, created picnic areas and provided bench seating throughout the grounds, including a circular seat around the willow tree by the main lake.

From the main Jersey Road entrance into the park, a long drive for cuts through two huge fields occupied by horses and cows. The farm shop at the end of the cowfield offers seasonal vegetables, all grown in the grounds. Wherever you find yourself within the park – the great meadow, the picnic area, pleasure grounds or the lakes –you can always see the four pineapple-shaped turrets of the main house, which act as a good guide should you ever feel lost.

The Pleasure Grounds are behind the main house, and are where summer events like open air theatre take place, as well as the annual Osterley Park poetry competition, which results in winning verses forming a poetry trail along the pebbled paths and among the sweeping trees of this garden. A walled area at the far end of the pleasure grounds reveals a series of well tended allotments. Back in front of the main house, the picnic area beside the lake is sometimes dotted with geese on the lookout for visitor's scraps. Stroll deeper into the woodlands at the south-eastern end of the park and you'll find the middle lake where fishing is available from June-March.

Richmond Park

Area: Approx 2,500 acres
Richmond, Surrey, TW10
Tel: 020 8948 3209
Transport: Richmond LU/Rail; Bus 371
Open: Daily 7am-dusk (Mar-Sept); daily 7.30am-dusk (Oct-Feb)
Facilities: Rugby pitches, football pitches, horse riding, cycle hire, fishing, polo, golf courses
Café

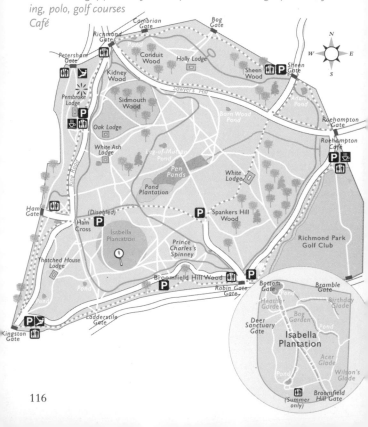

Cross country running, hill walking, cycling, horse-riding and pic-nicking all take place within the expanse of this Royal Park on the edge of south-west London, but it's the deer that are the biggest draw for the legions of visitors to Richmond Park. Red and fallow deer have grazed this land for centuries, and now have signs allow-ing them right of way across the roads that cut through the park. They've obviously come a long way since they were quarry for the royal court, Charles I having set the area aside for hunting in 1637. The monarch first came to the area in 1625, and holed up in Richmond Palace to escape the plague of that year which killed 35,000 people in London.

Richmond Park Cycle Hire (07050 209249) hires out two-wheelers for anyone wishing to take to the paths that surround the park. For sporty types, there is an area of grassland to the north of Roehampton Gate, with three winter rugby pitches, although at weekends its hired out exclusively to Rosslyn Park Rugby Football Club. The park also has fishing ponds and two 18-hole golf cours-es, as well as riding stables.

A designated Site of Special Scientific Interest and a Natural Nature Reserve, the park consists of meadows, open lawns, lush tree-lined paths and woodland. The park's central Isabella Plantation is a gorgeous organically run woodland garden with rich plant and flower life. Here you will find an enclosed playground, wooden bridges, streams, benches and shaded grassy areas that are perfect in the height of the summer.

Sustenance can be found at the Pembroke Lodge Café. This is a Georgian mansion, set within landscaped grounds, that was once the home of Bertrand Russell.

Richmond is a very green part of London and there are sever-al well preserved green spaces close to the park including Kew Botanical Gardens (see page 163), Hampton Court Palace and Gardens (see page 159), Bushy Park (see page 111) and Syon Park and Gardens (see page 166). Although the 2,500 acres of Richmond Park are usually enough for most visitors.

London's Gardens & Squares

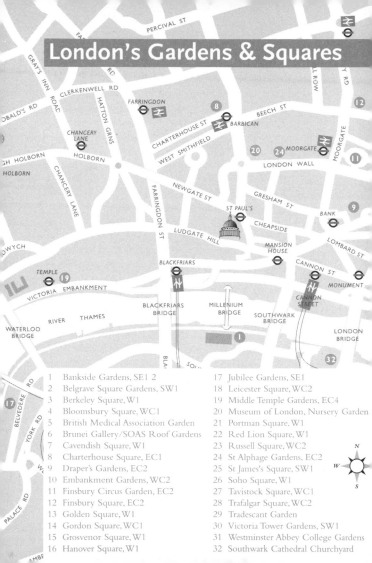

London's Gardens & Squares

This book would not be complete without some attention being paid to London's many squares and gardens. These small areas are not as dramatic or grand as the royal parks, but they are perhaps more useful, offering little oasis of calm amid the capital's noise and chaos. Cavendish Square is a great example of how useful such a green space can be – just a few minutes from Oxford Circus and yet offering grass lawns, trees and benches to the weary shoppers and office workers of the area.

Although gardens and squares serve the same vital service they vary greatly in their origins. The public gardens of London are the product of historical accident and vary as much in shape as they do in age. In contrast the squares of London are a creation of Georgian and Regency architecture and planning. The late 18th century was the time of London's expansion under the management of the land-ed gentry who developed vast areas of land in the Georgian style complete with elegant squares. John Nash continued this process with the patronage of the crown. All London's squares either date from this period or are built with reference to it.

London's gardens and squares are among its greatest assets and are a vital part of what makes London unique as a world city. Some of London's 600 gardens and Squares are listed in the following pages. The annual Garden Squares Weekend draws attention to the contribution that London's garden squares make to the capital's culture and environment.

London Open Garden and Squares Weekend

Website: www.opensquares.org
Open: Mid June annually
Run by the London Garden and parks Trust, this is the one weekend when many of London's private garden squares and other gardens open their gates to the public. A number of special activities take place in selected public gardens.

Central

Argyle Square, WC1
Transport: King's Cross LU

This modest square is just a few minutes walk from Kings Cross. It has a basketball court and enough trees and benches to make it a great place of escape from the traffic.

Bankside Gardens, SE1
Transport: Bank LU

Close to the Tate Modern, this garden on the south bank of the Thames has a central plaza, a lawn with birch trees and terraces surrounded by hedges.

Belgrave Square Gardens, SW1
Transport: Hyde Park LU

This circular garden in the middle of Belgrave Square has been restored to its original 19th-century layout with wisteria, roses and passion flowers. There's also a 'quiet garden' within the main garden.

Berkeley Square, W1
Transport: Green Park LU

Named after Lord Berkeley of Stratton, a civil war commander, this Mayfair enclave was built on the gardens of Devonshire House. It has a central garden of maple trees planted in the late 18th century.

Bloomsbury Square, WC1
Transport: Holborn or Russell Square LU

This square has kept some of its Georgian charm, with many fine surrounding buildings – although none of them original. The square itself is large with a broad paved area, lawns, a good selection of trees and plenty of benches. It's a great place to relax on a fine day when you've been shopping in Holborn. The most prominent feature of the square is the monument to Prime Minister Charles James Fox which was erected in 1816. There is also a blue plaque to Sir Hans Sloane, the benefactor of the British Museum, in the north-east corner of the square.

British Medical Association Council Garden

Tavistock Square, WC1, (0207 387 4499)
Transport: Euston LU/Rail or Russell Square LU

This garden with specially-grown physic plants is tucked away behind the south wing of BMA House. One of the walls has a plaque surrounded by stones from the foundation of the house that Dickens lived in from 1851-1860, and where he wrote *Bleak house*, *Hard Times* and *Great Expectations*. Also in the garden are a number of stones that were hit by incendiary bombs in April 1941.

Brunei Gallery/SOAS Roof Gardens

Russell Square (between Malet Street & Thornhaugh Street), WC1
(020 7898 4917)
Transport: Russell Square, Goodge Street, Euston Square and Tottenham Court Road LU, Euston LU/Rail

Opposite the main entrance to the School of Oriental and African Studies, the Brunei Gallery has a Japanese-style roof garden that was developed in 2001. Open during the gallery opening times, it offers a quiet retreat in the heart of Bloomsbury.

Calthorpe Project Community Garden

258-274 Gray's Inn Road, WC1 (020 7837 8019)
Transport: King's Cross LU/Rail

A community gardening resource set around a purpose built day centre and meeting venue. The central building's large verandas lead to the landscaped community gardens where activities from planting and weeding to composting take place. The organisation involves local schools in the maintenance of the garden as part of a series of ongoing community projects.

Soas Roof Garden

Cavendish Square, W1

Transport: Oxford Circus LU

This square was laid out for the 2nd Earl of Oxford in 1717 and is a small circular patch of green just to the north of Oxford Circus. On fine days the square is packed with people catching some sun and taking a break from the traffic. Past residents of the square include Captain Horatio Nelson.

Charterhouse Square, EC1

Transport: Barbican LU

The former site of Charterhouse public school, the square was built between 1700-1775. It still contains a few Georgian brick houses, some with their original ironwork and doorways.

Devonshire Square (off Cutler Street), EC2

Transport: Liverpool Street LU/Rail

This square still has a few of its original Georgian houses. It is one of the few quiet spaces around Liverpool Street and Aldgate and so very useful if you want to escape the crowds. The architecture is very fine, but those in search of vegetation will be disappointed as the square is paved.

Draper's Gardens, EC2

Transport: Bank LU

These gardens are behind Draper's Hall in Throgmorton Street, and represent only a small area of what once stretched all the way to London Wall. Although diminished in size the present gardens are still home to long established mulberry trees, one of which was planted by the Queen in 1955 and another by that royal lover of shrubbery Prince Charles in 1971.

Embankment Gardens, WC2

Including Temple Gardens, The Main Garden, Whitehall Garden and Whitehall Extension

Transport: Temple, Embankment LU

The Embankment Gardens are little known treasures extending along the north bank of the Thames and serving as little islands of calm amid the noise of Central London. Temple Gardens is just behind the Strand and directly outside Temple underground station. It is relatively small, but has lots of flower beds and mature trees as well as some fine monuments. The Main Garden is just in front of Embankment station and is a grand affair with many monuments and a very good café. Being located so near to Charing Cross it is a great way to escape the crowds. Whitehall Gardens lies beyond Northumberland Avenue and is perhaps the most beautiful of the gardens with three striking monuments and a great deal of lush plants and trees. The Whitehall Extension is a little barren by comparison, but is still worth a visit for the monuments it contains and for the view across the river to The London Eye.

Finsbury Circus Garden, EC2

Transport: Moorgate LU/Rail

One of the largest open spaces in the City, this circular garden is surrounded by modern, high tech architecture. Although the garden is rather sparse it does have a central bowling green and bands play here in the summer.

Finsbury Square, EC2

Transport: Moorgate LU/Rail

This large square is located just off City Road and close to the busy Old Street roundabout. The area is now very largely composed of modern office blocks but there are a few original Georgian buildings on the square. Those interested in London history will find the historic Bunhill Fields Burial Ground just a minutes walk north along City Road.

Golden Square, W1

Transport: Piccadilly Circus LU

Once known as Gelding's Close, this square was built between 1670-1700. It lies just north of Piccadilly, and is a great place to escape from the crowds which throng Regent Street and the area around the statue of Eros. The square itself is small and attractive with a few modest flower beds, a considerable expanse of paving, and a good number of benches. Standing in the middle of the square is a monument to George II which was erected during the monarchs reign. Charles Dickens refers to Golden Square in *Nicholas Nickleby*.

Gordon Square, WC1

Transport: Russell Square, Goodge Street LU

Close to Tavistock Square and also built by Thomas Cubitt. This was originally a private square for residents but is now owned by the University of London whose offices now occupy the surrounding grand buildings. The square is now open to the public with a large expanse of lawn and plenty of mature trees surrounding its borders.

Grosvenor Square, W1

Transport: Bond Street LU

The second largest square in London (after Russell Square), this area was designed and constructed between 1725-1731 by the Grosvenor Estate. The square is close to Hyde Park Corner and Oxford Street, but the lawns are dotted by tall tress with benches along the paths, making this a peaceful retreat from the bustle of central London. The sense of tranquility is only infringed by the United States Embassy which stands at the west end of the square surrounded by ugly concrete barriers and armed police. The square has a long association with the US and contains monuments to American presidents Franklin Roosevelt and Eisenhower and to the American and British fighter pilots of the Eagle Squadron of 1940.

Hanover Square, W1

Transport: Oxford Circus LU

The first of the Mayfair squares, Hanover Square is modest in size but lush and well maintained. It has Oxford Street to the north and Regent's Street to the east and is a great place to escape both busy thoroughfares. There is a monument to William Pitt the Younger.

Jubilee Gardens, SE1

Transport: Waterloo LU

This garden was established in 1977 to commemorate the Queen's Silver Jubilee. It is next to the London Eye and during the summer serves as a music venue. The garden is not particularly beautiful but does have great views of the Thames.

Leicester Square, WC2

Transport: Leicester Square LU

Famous for its cinema complexes and movie premieres, Leicester Square got its name from the second Earl of Leicester, who bought the land in 1630. It is one of the best known of London's squares and a popular rendezvous point. For this reason it is not a quiet place but a hive of activity with crowds, buskers and just a few token trees overshadowed by the cinema hoardings. Hogarth lived on the square and there's a bust of him as statues of Sir Isaac Newton, William Shakespeare and Charlie Chaplin.

Middle Temple Gardens, EC4

off Middle Temple Lane,
Transport: Temple LU
Open: May-July 11.30am-2.30pm

This very fine garden dates from the 12th century and derives its name from the Knights Templar residence that stood here. The gated garden offers well maintained herbaceous borders, roses, a fountain and fine trees surrounded by grand gothic buildings that serve as lawyers' chambers and apartments. Unfortunately the garden offers limited access to the public (see above) and can only be entered from the Strand via Middle Temple Lane. The other gardens along the Embankment are a better option (see page 127).

Museum of London, Nursery Garden, EC2

London Wall,
Transport: Barbican/St Paul's LU
Open: April-October 11.30am-2.30pm (Tuesday-Sunday)
Entry via the Museum of London

The museum's internal garden was redesigned in 1990 to coincide with an exhibition concerning the history of London's gardens and the nurserymen who worked in the capital. The garden contains a vast array of terracotta and royal blue pots containing a range of shrubs and plants including some plants found warmer climes.

Myddelton Square, EC1

Transport: Angel LU

The square is in the grounds of St Mark's Church, but is open to the public. It contains a playground for children, mature trees and plenty of benches. A great place to escape Islington's crowds.

Pimlico Gardens, SW1

Near St George's Square
Transport: Pimlico LU

This lush little space on the banks of the Thames is close to Vauxhall Bridge. It contains a monument to William Huskisson, the Victorian politician who was killed by a train having just declared the railway line open.

Portman Square, W1

Transport: Marble Arch LU

This square was developed in the late 18th century. The two and a half acre site includes well maintained hedges, shrubs and trees as well as a children's play area.

Russell Square

Red Lion Square, W1

Transport: Holborn LU

Named after a Holborn inn, this square was laid out in 1684. Although much has changed in Holborn the square remains a pleasant green space with lots of trees and shrubs and plenty of benches. Located just north of High Holborn and within walking distance of Oxford Street, it is a great place to escape the crowds. There are several monuments within the square including one to the philosopher Bertrand Russell who for a time lived on the square.

Riverside Walk Gardens, SW1

Between Millbank and Vauxhall Bridge
Transport: Pimlico LU

This garden was redesigned in 2004 with meandering paths, fibre-optic lighting and a Henry Moore sculpture entitled 'Locking Piece'. The resulting garden is minimalist in style and offers great views of the Thames.

Russell Square, WC2

Transport: Russell Square LU

The largest of London's Georgian squares was built on the grounds of Bedford House, in 1800. Its landmark building is the huge orange-bricked and elaborately styled Russell Hotel. The square itself is the only one to contain its own café which make it particularly popular with local office workers who flock here for an alfresco lunch. The squares other attractions include a central water fountain and a rather grand statue of the Duke of Bedford. In 2003 Russell Square was given a major refurbishment with improvements made to the fountain and new railings fitted. Author T.S. Eliot worked for nearly forty years for publishers Faber and Faber in Russell Square. In the mid 1930s, his wife Vivien, from whom he had separated, paraded outside the office with a sandwich board saying 'I am the wife that T.S. Eliot abandoned'.

St Alphage Gardens, EC2

Wood Street and Fore Street
Transport: Mansion House LU

This was once a churchyard and is now a public garden with the added attraction of a large chunk of Roman City Wall as a feature. The garden is a relatively narrow strip, built on two levels. The grass areas are lined with flower beds and benches with wooden steps leading to a lower garden and further on a small herb garden.

St James's Square, SW1

Transport: Piccadilly Circus LU

Laid out in the 1670s, this is one of London's oldest squares. It is small but well maintained and ideal for escaping the noise and traffic of Piccadilly. The square contains an imposing statue of William III astride a horse.

Soho Square, W1

Transport: Tottenham Court Road LU

Soho Square is a very popular green space with the office and shop workers of the area. On summer days it is often hard to find space to sit down. The square has stayed pretty much the same since the 1920s, with the paths and grass plots arranged around a central area where a statue of Charles II stood until recently. It has been replaced by a wooden arbour and tool shed. The singer Kirsty MacColl made mention of the square and a bench has been placed here in her memory.

Tavistock Square, WC1

Transport: Russell Square LU

This fine square was built by James Burton and Thomas Cubitt between 1803-26. Since those times the park's trees have reached maturity providing the contemporary visitor with plenty of shade. The square is associated with pacifism with a monument to Ghandi and a large stone commemorating conscientious objectors.

Trafalgar Square, WC2

Transport: Charing Cross LU/Rail

This square was laid out by John Nash in the 1820s and named to commemorate Nelson's victory at the Battle of Trafalgar (1805). Since that time the square has become a national meeting place where crowds gather to celebrate or protest. The square is dominated by Nelson's Column but there are many other monuments mainly to commemorate war heros such as Sir Henry Havelock. New developments to the north side of the area in 2003 mean there are now stairs leading to a large piazza in front of the National Gallery, instead of a busy road. Traffic is still very heavy around the square but it remains a pleasant place to visit if only to have a look at the monuments.

The Tradescant Garden at the Museum of Garden History, SE1

Lambeth Palace Road, (020 7401 8865)
Transport: Vauxhall or Lambeth North LU

The long disused Lambeth church that holds the grave of Captain Bligh has a garden at the back dedicated to the 17th-century father and son gardening duo (both called John Tradescant). The garden is laid out in geometric style with plants of that period.

Victoria Tower Gardens, SW1

Transport: Westminster LU

This large public garden stands between the Houses of Parliament and Lambeth Bridge. It contains a number of fine statues including a cast of Rodin's 'Burghers of Calais'. It is a great way to enjoy some peace from the traffic and crowds of Whitehall. Although interrupted by Parliament, Tower Gardens can be considered a continuation of the Embankment Gardens which extend along the Thames (see page 127).

The Tradescant Garden

Waterloo Millennium Green, SE1

Transport: Waterloo LU/Rail

This inner city green sits opposite the Old Vic Theatre in Waterloo, at the corner of Waterloo Road and Baylis Road. Once a run down adventure playground, it was redesigned in time for its 2000 reopening. It now features a fountain, wildflower and marsh gardens as well as children's playground.

Westminster Abbey College Gardens, SW1

Dean's Yard, (020 7222 5152)
Transport: St James's Park or Westminster LU

The garden of the famous medieval monastery was historically used to grow food and provide a peaceful place for the monks. Today's garden has a 17th-century style knot garden, a fig and mulberry tree and four statues of the Apostles which date from 1686.

North

Culpepper Community Gardens, N1

1 Cloudesley Street, (020 7833 3951)
Transport: Angel LU

A green oasis in the heart of Islington. Formerly a derelict site, it was developed in 1982 by the local community. They have turned it into an organic garden with around 46 plots, a pond, lawn, rose walkway and wildlife area.

West

Cadogan Place Gardens, SW1
Transport: Sloane Square LU

This fine garden dates from the 18th century and still has some of the original trees. It is a well tended green space and offers a welcome break from the shopping of Sloane Street.

Cleveland Gardens, W2
Transport: Bayswater LU

A quiet public garden surrounded by Bayswater's grand white stucco houses. Inside is a Japanese garden and children's play area.

Courtfield Gardens East, SW5
Transport: Earl's Court LU

A deep sunken garden with a miniature bog and an adjoining garden area to the west.

Ennismore Gardens, SW7
Transport: Knightsbridge LU

A short walk from Hyde Park and Kensington Gardens, this is a pleasant little green enclave. It contains an ornamental urn to commemorate Hollywood icon Ava Gardner, who lived for a time in nearby Ennismore Square.

Gloucester Square Garden, W2
Transport: Paddington LU/Rail

Beyond the urban environment of Paddington station sits this large English garden with flowerbeds, roses and mature plane trees.

Kensington Roof Gardens, W8

99 Kensington High Street (020 7937 7994)
Transport: High Street Kensington LU

With its entrance on Derry Street, the Roof Gardens were first landscaped in the 1930s. At 100 feet above street level they cover 1.5 acres and feature a Spanish garden, a Tudor garden, an English woodland garden and a pond with flamingos. The garden is an excellent vantage point for panoramic views of west London.

Ladbroke Square Garden, W11

Transport: Notting Hill Gate LU

The rectangular garden between Ladbroke Grove and Kensington Park Road is the largest of a series of tucked away green squares in the W11 area. It was the original site of the 19th-century Hippodrome Racecourse, which is now commemorated in nearby Hippodrome Place.

Queen's Gate Gardens, SW7

Transport: Gloucester Road LU

This fine Victorian garden is not far from The Natural History Museum and is a great place to escape the crowds of Kensington on fine days.

Rembrandt Gardens, W9

Warwick Avenue
Transport: Warwick Avenue LU

A well tendered little garden located next to the water network known as Little Venice. The garden has plenty of picnic tables from where you can enjoy the narrow boats that use the waterway.

Kensington Roof Garden

St George's Fields, W2

Gate in Albion Street
Transport: Marble Arch or Lancaster Gate LU

Just a few minutes walk from Marble Arch, this is a two and half acre woodland garden containing many unusual plants and trees. It is a wonderfully green place and well worth a visit - particularly on hot days when the shade is very welcome.

Victoria and Albert Garden, SW7

Cromwell Road (020 7942 2000)
Transport: South Kensington LU

What was once the Pirelli Garden at the V&A Museum will now simply be called the Victoria and Albert Garden. With a dashing new water feature, lemon trees and minus the large conifers that used to dominate, this garden now offers a huge space that connects with the museum's café and restaurant area.

South

Bonnington Square, SW8

Transport: Vauxhall LU/Rail

More a garden than a square, this quirky re-claimed bombsite was designed by Dan Pearson and James Fraser in 1994. It includes a 30-foot water wheel planted with wisteria, a boat, a walnut tree and tropical plant beds. The popular Bonnington vegetarian café is also part of the site.

Harleyford Road Community Garden, SE11

Transport: Vauxhall LU/Rail

Close to the Oval cricket ground, these gardens sprung up in 1984, when local residents started growing vegetables on the one and a half acres of wasteland. The garden now has a wildlife area, pond and children's play area.

Southwark Cathedral Churchyard, SE1

London Bridge
Transport: London Bridge LU/Rail

This garden is to the east of Southward Cathedral and is open to the public. It contains a sunken lawn, liquid amber trees and shrubs. The herb garden is often used by the cathedral's education centre and local schools visit to study the development of plants for medicinal use (020 7367 6700). The garden backs on to Borough Market which is the most popular food market in London and a magnet for London foodies.

East

Geffrye Museum Herb Garden, E2

Kingsland Road
Transport: Liverpool Street LU/Rail, Shoreditch LU
020 7729 5647

There are lawns in front of the Geffrye Museum, but the herb garden is a walled and gated former derelict site adjacent to the museum. It has a central bronze fountain and twelve beds filled with plants for cosmetic, medicinal, household or kitchen use. The garden is open to the public from April to October.

Ropemakers' Field, E14

Transport: Limehouse DLR

At the eastern end of the Regent's Canal, within a minutes walk of Limehouse Basin, lies this green space. The area was for centuries associated with London's maritime trade and its name derives from the many rope making workshops that existed here. This garden is a recent arrival having been laid out in the 1990s during the areas redevelopment. The space is well designed with plenty of park benches and a children's playground. It's a great place to catch your breath after a walk along the canal.

London's Landmarks

Greenwich

North

Alexandra Palace

Alexandra Palace Way, N22
Tel: 020 8365 2121
Website: www.alexandrapalace.com
Transport: Wood Green LU or Alexandra Palace Rail
then W33, 144, 184 bus
Open: Park open daily 24 hours;
Palace times vary depending on exhibitions
Admission free

Ally Pally has had more than its fair share of troubles during its lifetime. Triumphantly labelled as 'the people's palace' when it opened in 1873, it was built within its parkland setting to provide Victorian London with a spectacular leisure centre. These days, the Guy Fawke's night fireworks display is the biggest annual draw, although the palace is regularly used for exhibitions and conferences. Features include an indoor ice-skating rink and the boating lake and pitch and putt course in the summer. The palace is now set for a £3.5million redevelopment programme.

London Central Mosque

146 Park Road, NW8
Tel: 020 7724 333
Transport: Baker Street LU
Open: Daily 9.30am-6pm
Admission free

The golden dome of the London Central Mosque can be seen from all over **Regent's Park**. Designed by architect Frederick Gibberd, it was completed in 1978. Situated on the western edge of Regent's Park, the mosque is actually part of the Islamic Cultural Centre. It was built as a place of worship for the growing numbers of Muslim residents and visitors to London.

London Zoo

Outer Circle, Regent's Park, NW1
Tel: 020 7722 3333
Transport: Camden Town LU or Baker Street LU
Open: Summer daily 10am-5.30pm, winter daily 10am-4.30pm
(Closed Christmas Day)
Admission £10.75-£14

The London Zoo gives visitors the chance to observe over 650 species that live here, which include a varied range of reptiles, fish, invertebrates, birds and mammals, with around 112 of these listed as threatened species. With 36 acres to cover, it's difficult to know where to start, but a guidebook and map is available at the entrance for £3.50. Easily accessible by bus, train or tube, it's an even better experience to visit the zoo by river. The London Waterbus Company offers a boat trip and zoo entry package from Camden Lock, which takes you straight into the grounds. Call 020 7482 2550/2660 for details.

Regent's Park Open Air Theatre

Queen Mary's Gardens, Regent's Park, NW1
Tel: 020 7486 1933
Website: www.openairtheatre.org/
Transport: Camden Town LU

There's always a summer season of (mainly Shakespearean) plays at **Regent's Park's** famous theatre, which opens every year from the end of May to the beginning of September. First established in 1932, when thespian Sydney Carroll put on four matinées of Twelfth Night, it was in June the following year that Carroll and Lewis Schaverian were given a licence to formally open the theatre. The theatre was transformed in the 1960s and is now one of London's largest, with a 1,200 seating capacity. The present auditorium being built in 1975.

West

Fulham Palace

Bishop's Avenue, SW6
Tel: 020 7736 3233
Transport: Hammersmith or Putney Bridge LU
Open: Wed-Sun 2pm-5pm (March-Oct);
Thurs-Sun 1pm-4pm (Nov-Feb)
Admission: Call for details

There's said to have been a settlement here since 704AD. The palace has been rebuilt several times, although it remained the main residence of every Bishop of London up until 1973. Today's mixed styles are the result of constant re-structuring, and the now Grade I listed building has a red brick Tudor courtyard and Georgian façade on the east front. Tours of the interior and grounds of the palace usually take place every second Sunday, or once a month on a Wednesday. Tree walks can also be booked for garden visits. The palace lies in the middle of **Fulham Palace Botanical Gardens** (see page 54).

Holland House

Holland Walk, W8
Tel: 020 7937 0748
Transport: High Street Kensington LU
Restaurant

The remains of Holland House take centre stage inside **Holland Park** (see page 57). What exists today is essentially a shell of what survived after a series of bombings. Now, the former Jacobean mansion has a restored east wing where the Holland Park Youth Hostel has been since 1959. In the 1960s the house's Garden Ballroom was converted into a restaurant. During the summer there's a 10-week run of open-air theatre and ballet performances in the canopied Holland Park Theatre (020 7602 7856) at the front of the house.

Serpentine Gallery
Kensington Gardens, W2
Tel: 020 7402 6075
Website: www.serpentinegallery.org/
Transport: Lancaster Gate LU or South Kensington LU
Open: Daily 10am-6pm
Admission: free

Originally built as a tearoom in the 1930s, the Grade II listed building was converted to a gallery in 1970. Since that time the gallery has built up an impressive back list of high profile exhibitors including Henry Moore, Man Ray and Rachel Whiteread. Over 500,000 visitors each year come to browse in the arts bookshop, or take to the sleek exhibition spaces, that are a stark white contrast to the building's red brick exterior. Annually a contemporary architect or artist is given their first UK commission to design an outdoor pavilion. The space then becomes the location for a programme of open air events that run throughout June to September. See **Kensington Gardens** (page 12) for further details of the surrounding park.

Speakers' Corner
Hyde Park, W2
Tel: 020 7298 2100
Transport: Hyde Park Corner, Knightsbridge, Lancaster Gate or Marble Arch LU; Bus 2, 8, 10, 12, 23, 38, 73, 94

For over 150 years, Speakers' Corner at the Marble Arch end of **Hyde Park** has given many mouthy Londoners the chance to express their views to a public audience who can listen, heckle or move on to any other soap-boxed speakers. It is a type of verbal street theatre which draws crowds every Sunday come rain or shine. Historical figures who have spoken here include William Morris, George Orwell, Emmeline Pankhurst, Marcus Garvey and CLR James. It is worth remembering that in less liberal and democratic times this area was one of the sites for public execution known as *Tyburn*.

South-west

The Pump House Gallery

Battersea Park, SW11
Tel: 020 7350 0523
Transport: Sloane Square LU then 19 or 137 bus, Battersea Park or Queenstown Road Rail
Open: Wed, Thurs & Sun 11am-5pm; Fri & Sat 11am-4pm
Admission free

The tranquil lakeside setting of **Battersea Park's** Pump House Gallery makes it a perfect location for contemporary art exhibitions. The venue was built in 1861, but by the late 1940s it was a derelict ruin. In the 1980s, English Heritage took over the repairs and the gallery was reopening in 1992. Over the years, the gallery has hosted contemporary solo and group exhibitions from an international range of artists. The venue also works with schools, colleges, community groups and artists to produce exhibition talks and drop-in workshops.

South-east

Crystal Palace Museum

Anerley Hill, SE18
Tel: 020 8676 0700
Transport: Crystal Palace Rail
Open: Sun, Bank Holiday Monday 11am-5pm
Admission free

The Crystal Palace Museum is housed in an old engineering school at the Anerley Hill edge of the **Crystal Palace Park**. Open on Sundays and Bank Holiday Mondays only, and run by volunteers from the Crystal Palace Foundation, the museum's wares include videos and audio presentations, as well as artefacts from the original Crystal Palace exhibition. There are plans to upgrade the museum as part of the ongoing regeneration of the area.

National Maritime Museum

Romney Road, SE10
Tel: 020 8858 4422/8312
Website: www.nmm.ac.uk/
Transport: Cutty Sark DLR or Greenwich DLR/Rail
Open: Daily 10am-5pm
Admission free

One of the cluster of historical buildings within the setting of **Greenwich Park**, the National Maritime Museum keeps going from strength to strength in terms of its design and content. An impressive lawn-fronted entrance on Romney Road leads to a bright and airy lobby and a series of galleries offering permanent and temporary exhibitions on all things related to maritime history from Morse code to trade and expeditions. Three floors open up a world of seafaring delights, with galleries dedicated to Explorers, Passengers and Maritime London among other nautical themes.

Queen's House

Park Row, SE10
Tel: 020 8312 6565
Website: www.nmm.ac.uk/
Transport: Greenwich DLR/Rail or Maze Hill Rail
Open: Daily 10am-5pm
Admission free

This elegant Indigo Jones designing building sits next door to the NMM and is home to the permanent *Sea of Faces* exhibition, which features over 130 portraits of famous naval figures. The birthplace of Henry VIII and daughters Mary and Elizabeth has been sumptuously renovated in recent years. The grand interiors provide a fitting environment for National Maritime arts collection. The Tulip Staircase was the first to be built in this country and worth visiting in its own right. The staff are friendly, well informed and always willing to share their knowledge with visitors. A great place to visit in conjunction with **Greenwich Park** (see page 83).

The Royal Observatory & Planetarium

Greenwich Park, SE10
Tel: 020 8858 4422
Website: www.nmm.ac.uk/
Transport: Blackheath Rail or Greenwich DLR/Rail
Open: Daily 10am-5pm
Admission free

Part of the National Maritime Museum, the Royal Observatory sits in the centre of **Greenwich Park**, offering free entry to those wanting to visit the official home of Greenwich Mean Time and the Prime Meridian Line. The Observatory is the official starting point for each new day, year and Millennium, with the Meridian Line cutting through its courtyard. This enables visitors to place their feet on either side of it and to straddle two hemispheres. Time, space and cosmology are also explored through gallery exhibitions and in the domed Planetarium which sits behind the Observatory.

The Thames Barrier

1 Unity Way, Woolwich, SE18
Tel: 0208 854 1373
Website: www.thamesbarrierpark.org.uk/
Transport: North Greenwich LU or Charlton Rail
Open: Daily 10.30am-4.30pm (April-late September); daily 11am-3.30pm (Late Sept-March); closed 24 Dec-2nd Jan
Admission 50p-£1

Described as the eighth wonder of the modern world, this awesome example of design and engineering sits across the river from the **Thames Barrier Park** (see page 103), and is the world's largest movable flood barrier. The Thames Barrier has its own Learning and Information Centre on the south bank (call 020 8305 4188 for the programme of closures of the barrier gates). You can now stroll along the Thames Path which runs upstream from the Barrier and stretches to Richmond, although there are trains from Woolwich Arsenal, Plumstead and Erith if the walk gets too demanding.

East

Hackney City Farm

1a Goldsmith's Row, E2
Tel: 0207 729 6381
Website: www.hackneycityfarm.co.uk
Transport: Bethnal Green LU (then 15min walk); Bus 55, 48, 26
Open: Tues-Sun 10am-4.30pm
Admission free

Just on the edge of **Haggerston Park**, Hackney City Farm is home to geese, pigs, chicken, sheep and cattle, all living within urban E2. Visitors can get touchy-feely with the lambs in spring, when bottle-feeding sessions sometimes take place. Other activities like story-telling, circus skills, textile-making and cycling events happen every week. The organic garden is open for community planting or simply enjoying the scent of its aromatic herbs. It's an area of fruit trees, fruit bushes and deep flowered borders, as well as a large central vegetable patch. The farm's organic Frizzante Café serves great food.

Ragged School Museum

46-50 Copperfield Road, E3
Tel: 020 8980 6450
Website: www.raggedschoolmuseum.org.uk
Transport: Mile End LU
Open: Wed & Thurs 10am-5pm, First Sun of every month 2pm-5pm
Admission free
Café

A visit to **Mile End Park** (see page 99) wouldn't be complete without taking in this shrine to east London history. The Ragged School Museum building started life as a canalside warehouse before becoming a school for local poor children. The building lay derelict for some time before being reopened as a local museum in 1990. It's a great place to hear about the stories of local people and is run with enthusiasm by a team of volunteers.

London's Other Green Spaces

Chelsea Physic Gardens

Gated Parks & Gardens

Chelsea Physic Gardens

Area: Approx 4 acres
66 Royal Hospital Road, (entrance at Swan Walk), SW3
Tel: 020 7352 5646
Website: www.chelseaphysicgarden.co.uk
Transport: Sloane Square LU
Open: Wed 12noon-5pm, Sun 2pm-6pm (April-Oct),
Admission: £3-£5 (check website for tour details)
Café

One of Europe's oldest botanical gardens, the Chelsea Physic Garden offers a perfect respite from the jarring sounds of the city. Nowhere near the scale of the mammoth botanical gardens at Kew, this is a bijou space in comparison, and was founded in 1673 by the Society of Apothecaries, who wanted to study the healing effects of plants. Today the place is far more of an ornamental garden than a botanical one, with regular walks, dance and story-telling sessions for children, resident poets and a teahouse café.

There's a broad collection of medicinal plants from the tropical and sub-tropical Mediterranean regions and the Canary Islands. The ethnobotanical garden of world medicine has spawned some innovative projects, including an initiative with Moroccan women from the nearby Al-Hasanyia community centre, who've shared their wide-ranging knowledge of North African plants.

It's the garden's south-facing position that creates a warm micro-climate that suits the rare and exotic plants that thrive here. These include the largest outdoor olive tree in Britain, and one of the oldest rock gardens in Europe. Another claim to fame is the 1817 discovery of forced rhubarb at the site – when rhubarb plants left covered in a bucket, developed tender stems and curling yellow leaves, which inspired a legion of copycat gardeners. The statue of one of botanist, Hans Sloane (see picture opposite) is worth paying homage to, not least because he is the inventor of chocolate.

155

Hampton Court Park

HAMPTON COURT ROAD

Wilderness
House

Lion
Gate

HAMPTON COURT WAY

Maze

The Wilderness

Nursery

P

North Canal

Fountain
Garden

The Barge Walk

West
Front

Hampton Court
Palace

Orangery

Long Wa

HAMPTON
COURT

Landing
Stage

Great
Vine

Sunken
Gardens

Privy
Garden

Banqueting
House

Thames

South Canal

N
W   E
S

Hampton Court Park

Area: Approx 60 acres
East Molesey, Surrey, KT8
Tel: 0870 751 5175/0870 752 7777
Website: www.hrp.org.uk
Transport: Hampton Court Rail; riverboat from Westminster or
Richmond to Hampton Court Pier
Open: Palace Mon 10.15am-6pm, Tues-Sun 9.30am-6pm (April-Oct);
Mon 10.15am-4.30pm, Tues-Sun 9.30am-4.30pm (Nov-March); Park
open dawn til dusk daily
Admission: Palace, courtyard and maze £7-£11.80
Café

The exceptionally well-coiffured 60 acres of Hampton Court Park, with pristine gardens, arbours, tree-lined walks and woodland areas, surrounds the famous royal palace. With over 500 years of royal history behind it, this is a far more gentile affair than the unkempt expanse of nearby Bushy Park (see page 111).

A heady mix of Dutch, Italian and French design influences, the gardens date from the 17th century. The riverside gardens include the famous maze with its half a mile of paths and a soundscape, which was installed in spring 2005 – perhaps to calm any visitors who get lost within the surprisingly complex series of hedges. Established in 1690, this was Britain's first hedge-planted maze, although the current plot is all that remains of the original. It was so well loved, that by the time royal gardener Capability Brown came to the palace in the 18th century, he was expressly forbidden from making any changes to it. This must have been a frustrating state of affairs given his anti-formal design style and the fact that he lived next to the maze for twenty years. These days, the maze gets somewhere around 300,000 visitors a year who generally take about twenty minutes to half an hour to negotiate the labyrinth - although there are a few lost sheep that take a lot longer

Costumed guides offer free tours of the palace, and there are talks during the summer by gardeners, housekeepers, flower

159

arrangers and the vine keeper. The latter has a busy time tending the palace's Great Vine, which was planted in 1768, and is the largest in the world at over 120 feet long. It is capable of producing a bumper 600 pounds of black grapes a year, which are sold to visitors. This enterprising spirit is nothing new. Hampton Court has a tradition of grape trading that goes back nearly one-hundred years to King George V's reign. He started sending grapes to hospitals before eventually selling them to the palace visitors.

Avenues of lime trees, lakes and a sunken water garden dating back to Henry VIII's residency keep up the parks' regal status. Further attractions include the Fountain Garden, with its neat lines of umbrella-shaped yews and the Long Water – the artificial lake that runs parallel to the Thames. This area forms one of three garden areas around the palace. The others include the less formal Northern gardens with mixed hedges, herbaceous borders, a wilderness area and the much-visited Maze, and then there's the South gardens with a series of sunken pond areas, the Knot Garden and the famous Privy Garden. The Privy Garden was completed for William III in 1702 and restored in 1991-1995, using the same varieties of plants that were originally grown there. Beyond the formal gardens lies the extensive parkland which is an open area of oak trees and deer.

At one time, entrance to the park and gardens was free. Now that Hampton Court Palace is run as a charity a fee has been introduced to fund the maintenance necessary to keep the place open to the public. Palace tickets include automatic access to the gardens and maze. Admission is £4 (adults) and £2.50 (children) to visit the grounds at the back of the palace, which include the Privy Garden and the Great Vine. It is still free for those visiting the park areas and avoiding the palace and its gardens.

London Wetland Centre

Queen Elizabeths Walk, SW13
Tel: 020 8409 4400
Website: www.wwwt.org.uk/visit/wetlandcentre/
Transport: Hammersmith LU then 33, 72, 209 bus
Open: Summer daily 9.30am-6pm; Winter daily 9-30am-5pm
Admission: £4-£6.75

One of nine UK conservation centres run by the Wildfowl and Wetland Trust, the London Wetland Centre opened in May 2000, and earned itself a Site of Special Scientific Interest (SSSI) award by 2002. The first project of its kind in the world, its 105 acres have been carved out in an area that's just four miles from central London, and gives its hordes of visitors a chance to observe the growing populations of rare or threatened wildlife that thrive on the site's open water, lakes, mudflats and reedbeds.

The whole area is dotted with various indoor and outdoor features including a function room for corporate events, and a state-of-the-art 3-screen cinema showing *Planet Water* — a short film about the London Wetland Centre and the work of the WWT. The art gallery is another of the centre's indoor options, displaying work by wildlife and landscape artists, usually through seven different exhibitions a year.

Near the edge of the lakes the three-storey Peacock Tower provides a panoramic view of the reserve and the expanse of marshland where wildfowl like wigeon, lapwing, and snipe regularly graze. There's also a pristine split-level heated bird airport (or observatory), that gives an excellent view of the main lake and London skyline.

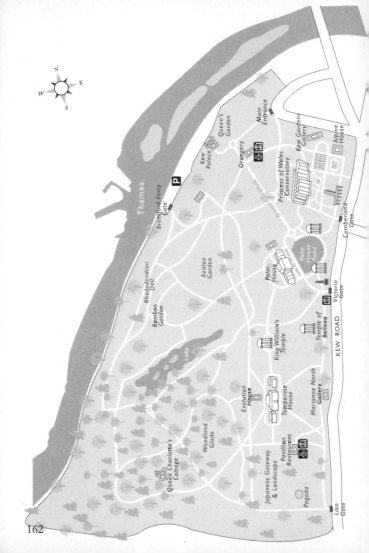

Royal Botanic Gardens at Kew

Area: Approx 300 acres
Kew, Richmond, TW9
Tel: 020 8332 5000
Website: www.rbgkew.org.uk
Transport: Kew Gardens LU/Rail or Kew Bridge Rail; riverboat to Kew Pier
Open: Mon-Fri 9.30am-6.30pm, Weekend & Bank hols 9.30am-7.30pm (April-Aug); Daily 9.30am-6pm (Sept-Oct); Daily 9.30am-4.15pm (Nov-Jan); Daily 9.30am-5.30pm (Feb-Mar)
Admission: £6.50-£11.75
Café/restaurant

For the last two centuries, hundreds of gardeners and researchers have converged on this green oasis on the south-west bank of the Thames. The site's botanical garden was declared a World Heritage Site by Unesco in 2003. Combined with this international reputation, Kew is also a major visitor attraction with art-spaces, educational resources and access to the gardens. It also has a rolling programme of festivals and other live events.

The garden's most famous attractions are the Amazonian water lilies, and the plants in the steamy palm house. This includes the Chilean vine palm, raised from a seed collected in Chile in 1846, and the world's tallest indoor plant. A giant bamboo is said to grow up to a metre a day, and then there's the strychnos tree, which produces a deadly poison used in hospitals to paralyse patients' muscles during surgery. The Temperate House plays host to the world's largest permanent orchid display, with one resident's petals growing to an impressive three feet in length.

The Kew Gardens experience can involve hanging out in a rainforest, strolling down huge tree-lined avenues, stepping through a desert-like landscape or picking your way through allotments. Containing around ten percent of the world's flowering plant species, it even has its own police force – perhaps as a warning to any light-fingered visitors who are after some cuttings.

There's a lot to see here, which can be a bit daunting if you're considering where to start. Unless you've got something specific that you want to see, it's probably best not to plan, and to stumble across the different features and hidden away areas as you find them.

Recently, a Morphine Poppy field was planted at the Thames end of the gardens – permission was given by the Home Office – and other fine features include a series of modern gardens created by horticultural students. Kew's educational role is channelled through a wide programme that includes teacher guidance that's available through *www.rbgkew.org.uk* or by calling 020 8332 5655.

The Great Pagoda is another popular landmark within the grounds. Built in 1762, it is now sadly too shaky for visitors to enter. If you want a great view of Kew, just west of the pagoda is the aerial tree walk, which leads to the top of a giant redwood. From here you can survey the lush forest canopy and beyond.

The Marianne North Gallery is located at the eastern border of the gardens. It looks a bit like a red-brick community centre, but inside the rooms are packed with over 800 lively paintings by Marianne North, a 19th-century traveller, with a passion for painting plants. She presented her artwork to Kew and had this gallery built for the purpose, while she hot-footed it off to South Africa, the Seychelles and Chile.

In mid 2005, the Field Hospital pavilion opened within the gardens, and has become a centre of research into herbal healing. Here researchers trace the science behind many an 'old wives tale', with the medicinal properties of figwort (a wound healer), basil (a treatment for Parkinson's disease), leech saliva (for post-operative swelling) and others all coming under the microscope.

There's a huge amount of ground to cover, from the elaborate glass houses to the herbaceous gardens. If you're not up to walking your way around, you can book a ticket on the Kew Explorer. An eco-friendly gas-powered road train, it runs from the garden's Victoria Gate, and provides a laid back 35-minute tour of the site, allowing passengers to jump on and off when they like.

Kew Gardens

Syon Park and Gardens

Area: 200 acres
Syon Park, Brentford, Middlesex, TW8
Tel: 020 8560 0882
Aquatic Experience 020 8847 4730
London Butterfly House 020 8560 7272
Website: www.syonpark.co.uk
Transport: Gunnersbury LU/Rail then 237, 267 bus
Open: Gardens 10.30am-5pm daily. Closed 25 & 26 December
Admission: House & Gardens £7.50; Gardens £3.75

The well-manicured lawns, neatly-trimmed hedges and rare trees within the walled grounds of Syon Gardens give a definite sense of being in an exclusive setting. Peacocks, a central lake framed by willows and snoozing ducks all add to the pleasure of visiting this historic house and its landscaped gardens beside the Thames, about ten miles from central London.

Home to the Duke of Northumberland's family for over 400 years, Syon was named after Israel's Mount Zion. The house is built on the site of a medieval abbey that Henry VIII eventually destroyed. This wasn't too popular at the time, but he received divine payback in 1547, when his coffin was brought to Syon on its way to Windsor for burial. It is said that the box burst open during the night, and in the morning dogs were found licking up Henry's remains.

The 200 acre park has all kinds of appealing features. The garden area was first established in the mid-16th century and occupies about thirty acres. It was re-landscaped in the 18th century by royal gardener Capability Brown, who introduced two lakes, one of which is now used for trout fishing.

The garden at the front of the house has 100 different types of roses, which create a perfect medley of colours in the summer. An ice house stills stands, although it's no longer used for the same purpose as when it was built in the 1760s to store ice from the lake for the Duke's table.

The park's centrepiece is the Great Conservatory. A definite eye-catcher, it was commissioned by the 3rd Duke of Northumberland in 1826, and was the first of its type to be built out of gun metal, Bath stone and glass. It was a fancy bauble for the Duke to show off his exotic plants, and served as an inspiration for Joseph Paxton when he was putting together his own designs for the Crystal Palace.

Wedding receptions, TV, magazine and film shoots regularly use the Syon landscape, with Gosford Park (2001), Emma (1996) and The Madness of King George (1994) being some of the better-known period movies to have filmed here.

The London Butterfly House is another firm favourite among the Park's attractions. Opened in 1981, it's a warm glasshouse where visitors can walk freely amongst the hundreds – if not thousands – of free-flying tropical butterflies that live there.

There's also the Aquatic Experience, which is an exhibition of rescued or endangered species that live in the rain forests. Piranhas, snakes, crocodiles and marine toads are all based in this tropical environment that includes cascading waterfalls and lush plants. You have to pay separately for the various features within the gardens, which bumps up the price of a visit, but you are at least paying for something that's out of the ordinary.

Commons

Barnes Common, SW13

Area: Approx 120 acres
Church Road, SW13
Tel: 020 8878 2359
Transport: Stamford Brook or Ravenscourt Park LU and Mortlake or Chiswick Rail
Facilities: Cricket pitch and football pitch

This green area is close to the starting point of the annual Oxford and Cambridge boat race at Mortlake. It covers around 120 acres, which in the 16th century, were shared between the villages of Barnes and Putney. That is, until 1589, when a dispute broke out between the two communities, which led to the barring of the common to Putney residents. By the second half of the 19th century, the common, a huge expanse of marshland, was used for research by naturalists. Nowadays, it's separated from Lower Putney Common by Common Road, but its cricket and football grounds are still well-used.

Barnes Common has a place in the annals of rock, being the site of pop star Marc Bolan's fatal car crash in 1977. Flowers and ribbons still mark the spot to this day, and to commemorate the twenty-fifth anniversary of the musician's death, a bronze bust was unveiled beside the site by his son Rolan Bolan.

Designated as a local nature reserve in 1992, the 40 acre common is a great area for spotting green woodpeckers and rare flowers including white-flowered burnet roses that usually make an appearance during the summer.

Clapham Common, SW4

Area: Approx 220 acres
Clapham Common, Clapham High Street, SW4
Transport: Clapham Common, Clapham North and Clapham South
LU or Clapham High Street Rail
Facilities: Rugby pitch, football pitch, tennis courts, basketball court,
fishing ponds, bowling green
Café

Perhaps it's thanks to former MP Ron Davies' 'moment of madness' in 1998, that Clapham Common is still shaking off a reputation as an after hours cruising ground. This is a long way from its origins as a peaceful pasture, where animals grazed on the land right up to the early 20th century. In fact, before the landscape was tamed the common was a hangout for 17th-century highwaymen, including the 'notorious sinner' Robert Forrester. He dressed in ladies' clothes to fool those travelling in passing stagecoaches.

The origins of the common date back to Saxon times, when the land contained a small settlement known as Osgod Clapha, which remained an isolated hamlet for many centuries. It wasn't until the end of the 17th century, when the Fire of London, made many Londoners homeless, that the south-west of the city became a popular place to live. At times the wildlife of the common encroached on the human dwellings and rewards of ten shillings were paid for all those who could kill a decent amount of hedgehogs or polecats.

By the 18th and 19th centuries the common was surrounded by grand houses belonging to City merchants, philanthropists, and the likes of diarist Samuel Pepys who lived here from 1700 to 1703.

Today, many bars, shops and restaurants surround the west and south sides of the common. The common now feature open grassland areas, woodlands, tree-lined paths and three ponds – two with fishing areas and one for model boats. There are areas for rugby, tennis, basketball and football, and each summer the Clapham Festival takes place with fêtes, comedy shows, the Gay Queen of Clapham contest, film screenings and live music.

Tooting Common

Area: 221 acres
Tooting Bec Road, SW16 & SW17
Transport: Balham and Tooting Bec LU
Facilities: Athletics track, fishing (membership required), horse riding,
lido, tennis courts, sports pitches, One O'clock Club
Café

This 150 acre open space is the remnant of a piece of open land that once stretched as far as Mitcham. Tooting Bec Common was one of the first commons to be preserved by the Metropolitan Board of Works in the late 19th century.

One of its biggest draws is the art deco Lido – the largest in Europe – that was first built in 1906. Every summer, crowds flock to this swimming pool, which has a paddling area, and café. The Lido opens every Christmas Day to allow local masochists the chance to swim in arctic conditions.

The rest of the landscape is made up of woodland, open grassland and sports areas. There's a fine path of oak trees along Dr Johnson Avenue, which splits the main common from the smaller Tooting Graveney Common just beyond the tennis courts. These trees were planted in the late 16th century to commemorate a visit by Elizabeth I. The avenue was named after the 18th-century writer Samuel Johnson, who was a regular visitor to his friend Henry Thrale, whose house overlooked the common.

Other avenues within the common have horse chestnuts or elms lining them, and there's an old Keeper's Lodge at the end of Dr Johnson Avenue that was built in 1879.

Not far from the junction of Tooting Bec Road and Elmbourne Road at the far south western edge of Tooting Graveney, there's an old yachting pond. Close by are a series of sculptures that were carved out of trees damaged in the great storm of 1987.

Wandsworth Common

Area: 175 acres
Trinity Road, SW11 and SW18
Tel: 020 8874 1841
Transport: Balham and Clapham South LU; Clapham Junction,
Wandsworth Town or Earlsfield Rail
Facilities: Sports pitches, tennis courts, bowling green, fishing

Both Wandsworth and Clapham Common are often referred to by locals as 'Nappy Valley' as they both seem to be residential magnets for young families. Wandsworth Common's 175 acres stretch from the edges of Balham to Battersea Rise, with a history that goes right back to the 11th century. Back then, there were public rights on the common to cut wood or shrubs, graze animals and cultivate the land. This all changed when London started expanding and created new pressure to develop the area. Gradually large chunks of the common passed into private hands, and the area was divided by new road and rail links. By 1887, the common was a muddy, treeless expanse that needed new public attention.

Today, it's a different story. Edged by 19th century and Edwardian houses, the common is as it should be – a sprawling green space with sports pitches, tennis courts, bowling greens and ornamental areas. On Windmill Road, there's a boarded wind pump, which was built in 1840 to revive the common's water supply. It's been redundant since 1870, and now has Grade II listed status.

The Scope is a 25-acre section of the common that's specifically managed for wildlife with oaks, silver birch, woodland and grassland found here. It's also home to the Environment Centre (020 8871 3863) – a privately-run charity that offers various nature and wildlife activities for visitors of all ages. Of the common's two lakes, one is for fishing (seasonal membership is required), the other is a parkland feature known as Three Island Pond. In the past year this lake was given a complete overhaul, which introduced cleaner water and a range of waterside plants.

Wimbledon Common

Area: Approx 1,140 acres
Windmill Road, SW18
Transport: East Putney, Wimbledon Park and Southfields LU;
Wimbledon LU/Rail
Facilities: Cricket pitch, football and rugby pitches, golf course, horse riding, nature trail

This common is huge. Its unenclosed acres (all 1,140 of them) are divided by the A3 and bounded on the east side by Wimbledon Park. The huge area, which peters out where Wimbledon Common joins Richmond Park, is almost twice the size of Hampstead Heath.

Its facilities include playing fields, cottages, two golf courses, gravel pits, woodlands, sixteen miles of horse rides, warrens, camp areas, lakes and ravines. Two thirds of the common have been designated as a Site of Special Scientific Interest (SSSI) as well as a Special Area of Conservation (SAC). There's plenty to see, with a landscape that features unenclosed and unspoilt grassland areas and multiple paths leading to further open or wild areas.

Towards Putney Heath at Windmill Road, the old windmill has been standing here since 1817. It is thought to be the UK's only remaining example of a hollow-post flour mill. Built by a carpenter, Charles March, it was working up until 1865, before eventually becoming a residential property. By 1975, it had been restored and it now operates as the Windmill Museum★, where grain grinding and other activities are offered for children.

The size of Wandsworth Common and the miles of track make it one of the best places around London to take a mountain bike for a decent ride. This is also the only way to cover the vast acreage of the common unless you are an equestrian with access to a horse.

★The Windmill Museum Windmill Road, SW19 (020 8947 2825) Wimbledon/East Putney tube or Wimbledon/Putney rail.
Open Fri 11am-5pm, Sat 2pm-5pm, Sun 11am-5pm, admission £1 adults, 50p children.

172

Peckham Rye Common

Area: 64 acres
Peckham Rye, SE15 & SE22
Transport: Peckham Rye, East Dulwich and Nunhead Rail

Angels and chocolate have an indelible link with this 64 acre of common land. It's where Elizabeth Cadbury, the Quaker wife of the chocolate manufacturer once lived, and is also the site where the poet William Blake claims he saw a vision of angels in an oak tree on the rye. The common surrounds the 49-acre Peckham Rye Park (see page 90), which opened up to the public in 1894. Not as intricately designed as the inner park, which has undergone significant restoration over the last two or three years, the wider green area does have children's playgrounds, leafy glades and a stream running along its edge.

Streatham Common

Area: 36 acres
South of Streatham Common and
North Crown Road (A214), SE15 & SE22
Transport: Streatham Rail

Of Streatham's 70 acres of green spaces, the common is the largest. Its 36 acres lie on the southern edge of the Streatham area, and stretch up towards Norwood from the High Road. Tucked within it is the four-acre walled Streatham Rookery (see page 66) with its themed gardens.

The common was once part of a large swathe of land stretching from Norbury to Tulse Hill, with a scattering of ponds, which were fed by a series of springs from Norwood via Beulah Spa, near Crystal Palace. The area had a long tradition of cricket matches during the 18th and 19th centuries, with those who were grand enough to have their houses situated around the edges of the land, having private access gates to the sports fields. Obviously there's still plenty of room for sports, but no particular activity takes precedence. There's a playground and an empty paddling pool, which now works pretty well as a place for small children to practice their bike skills.

Events happen throughout the year, and these are usually organised by the Friends of Streatham Common, who arrange regular funfairs. The annual Kite Day takes place every April and is open to flyers of all manner of kites from sello-taped bin bags to well-crafted aerodynamic constructions.

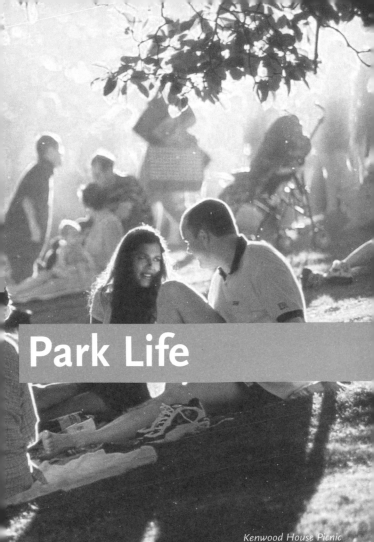

Park Life

Kenwood House Picnic

Cafés

Napoleon talked of an army 'marching on its stomach' and the same can be said of those trekking through London's parks and gardens – without the guns and needless slaughter. Just occasionally friends persuade me to visit the countryside and trudge through thoroughed fields without an herbaceous border in sight and, worst of all, no convenient place to sit and have a cappuccino. Acknowledging my love of the urban green space (where nature has been tamed), I include here some of the best cafés to be found in London's parks.

Holland Park Café

Brew House

Kenwood House, Hampstead Lane, NW3
Tel: 020 8341 5384
Transport: Kentish Town LU, Gospel Oak or Hampstead Heath Rail;
Bus 214, C2, C11
Open: April-Sept daily 9am-6pm (7.30pm on concert nights),
Oct-Mar daily 9am-4pm

It gets very busy at this former stable block at Kenwood House. Huge slabs of cake, hot drinks and sturdy English-style meals are what the Brew House is best known for.

Broadwalk Café & Playcafé

Kensington Gardens, W8
Tel: 020 7034 0722
Transport: Bayswater, High Street Kensington, Lancaster Gate or
Queensway LU; Bus 9, 12, 28, 49, 148
Open: Summer daily 8am-8pm, winter daily 10am-4pm.

This café is next to the Diana Memorial Playground and serves freshly cooked meals, salads, sandwiches and fair trade tea and coffee. There's a children's menu and outdoor seating.

Brockwell Park House

Brockwell Park, SE24
Tel: 020 7926 6200
Transport: Herne Hill Rail
Open: Daily 8am-4pm

Now a Grade II listed building, this once grand Regency mansion is now a faded house on a hill. The place is now well loved for its all day breakfasts, Italian ice creams, hot drinks, cakes and no-nonsense staff.

Crystal Palace Café

Crystal Palace Park, Thicket Road, SE20
Tel: 020 8778 9496
Transport: Crystal Palace Rail
Open: Daily 8am-4pm

In the area between the information centre and the dinosaur park, this friendly café serves chips, big mugs of tea, cakes, fry-ups and other stodgy delights.

The Dell

Eastern side of the Serpentine
Tel: 020 7706 0464
Transport: Hyde Park Corner LU
Open: 9am-8pm in the summer, 10am-4pm in the winter.

The dell has a large outdoor seating area (terrace and garden) and serves a wide selection of food and drink. It has the added advantage of being housed in a building by the modernist architect Patrick Gwynne on a site overlooking the Serpentine.

The Garden Café

Regent's Park, NW1
Tel: 020 7935 5729
Website: www.thegardencafe.co.uk
Transport: Baker Street LU or Regent's Park LU
Open: Mon-Fri 10am-6pm; Sat, Sun 9am-7pm

Next to the rose gardens and close to the park's Open Air Theatre, this recently refurbished café has a stylishly 1960s-retro look. There is a takeaway counter packed with goodies for picnics, and a smart indoor dining area. It is the family friendly garden terrace, with seating for 150 and table service, that is the real draw. Here you can enjoy the all day menu and they also serve alcohol which is rare for a park café.

Golders Hill Park Refreshment House

Hampstead Heath, off North End Road, NW5
Tel: 020 8455 8010
Transport: Kentish Town LU, Gospel Oak or Hampstead Heath Rail;
Bus 214, C2, C11
Open: Daily 10am-6pm

This family-run café offers pasta meals and salads as well as its famous Italian ice creams. The place is very popular with locals with queues in the summer.

The Honest Sausage

The Broadwalk, near London Zoo
& On the Meridian line, next to The Royal Observatory, Greenwich
Tel: 020 7935 5729
Website: www.honestsausage.com
Transport: Greenwich LU and Regent's Park LU
Open: 9am-8pm in the summer, 10am-4pm in the winter

Free range sausages and bacon in organic bread, organic fair trade tea and coffee. There is also a range of vegetarian options.

Inn the Park

St James's Park, SW1
Tel: 020 7451 9999
Transport: St James's Park LU; Bus 3, 11, 12, 24, 53, 211
Open: Daily 8am-11pm

Eat inside or outside at this eco-friendly café and restaurant that opened in April 2004. The wooden building was designed by Sir Michael Hopkins and has a turfed roof and a glass front. The kitchen is run by renowned chef Oliver Peyton and is equally innovative with touches like picnic hampers for those who want to eat in the park. The restaurant's menu changes from season to season, but is always consistently good with plenty of vegetarian options. The Cauliflower soup and goats cheese and leek flan are just some of the appetising choices.

La Gondola al Parco Restaurant

Battersea Park, SW11
Tel: 020 7720 0831/020 7978 1655
*Transport: Battersea Park or Queenstown Road Rail, Sloane Square
LU; Bus 9, 137*
Open: Mon-Fri 10am-5pm, Sat & Sun 8.30am-5pm

This family-run lakeside café serves portions of chunky chips, pasta dishes, salads and has live jazz on Tuesdays.

Lido Café

Hyde Park, W2
Tel: 020 7706 7098
*Transport: Hyde Park Corner, Knightsbridge, Lancaster Gate or
Marble Arch LU; Bus 2, 8, 10, 12, 23, 38, 73, 94*
Open: Summer daily 9am-8pm, winter daily 10am-4pm

Hyde Park's public pool has its own café on the south side of the Serpentine, next to the Lido swimming area. There are great views across the lake, alfresco eating or indoor dining and selections of newspapers to read while you sample the snacks or full meals.

The Orangery

Kensington Palace, Kensington Gardens, W8
Tel: 020 7376 0239
*Transport: Bayswater, High Street Kensington, Lancaster Gate or
Queensway LU; Bus 9, 12, 28, 49, 148*
Open: Daily 10am-6pm (Mar-Oct), Daily 10am-5pm (Nov-Dec)

You expect something fairly refined if you're eating in Kensington Gardens, and the Orangery doesn't disappoint. Cream teas include cucumber sandwiches and scones with jam and clotted cream. Freshly baked cakes are also on offer, as well as hot English meals at lunchtimes.

Osterley Park Tea Room

off Jersey Road, Isleworth, Middlesex, TW7
Tel: 020 8232 5057
Transport: Osterley LU
Open: Sat & Sun 11.30am 5pm (March), Wed-Sun 11.30am-5pm
(April-Oct including Bank Holidays and Good Friday), Wed-Sun
12noon-4pm (Nov-Dec)

This tearoom in the park's stable yard area offers coffee, tea, lunches and snacks. The menu uses home-grown vegetables from the park's farm.

Pavilion Café

Dulwich Park, College Road, SE21
Tel: 020 8299 1383
Transport: North Dulwich or West Dulwich Rail
Open: Daily 9am-5.45pm (summer), Daily 8.30am-dusk (winter)

On hot days, this glass-fronted café is opened up to allow full appreciation of the park surroundings – and some ventilation. Sweets and snacks are popular fayre, although there are also hot meals.

Pavilion Coffee Shop

Thames Barrier Park, Barrier Point Road,
off North Woolwich Road, E16
Tel: 020 7511 4111
Transport: Canning Town LU/DLR then 474 bus,
Stratford LU; Bus 69
Open: Fri-Sun 10am-4pm (occasionally other week days)

The state-of-the-art Visitor Pavilion in this 21st-century park is a vision of etched glass, oak frames and iroko decking, with indoor pinewood tables and chairs for comfortable seating. Coffee here comes from Africa, Asia and Latin America and there are also croissants, cakes and other snacks.

Pavilion Tea House

Charlton Way, SE10
Tel: 020 8858 9695
Transport: Cutty Sark DLR, Greenwich DLR/Rail, Maze Hill Rail;
Bus 1, 53, 177, 180, 188, 286; riverboat to Greenwich Pier
Open: Mon-Fri 9am-6pm, Sat & Sun 9am-7pm

A fine art deco style building near the park's Royal Observatory, where breakfasts, snacks, soups and gorgeous meals such as grilled salmon are served. Inside seating is on two levels, outside there are seats in the surrounding garden area.

Pembroke Lodge

Richmond Park, Richmond, Surrey, TW10
Tel: 020 8940 8207
Transport: Richmond LU/Rail; Bus 371
Open: Daily 10am-5.30pm (summer), daily 10am-5pm (winter)

At one time this Georgian mansion was the home of philosopher Bertrand Russell. It's now a café with extensive park views and a banqueting room capable of holding up to 130 people. There are seats in the garden, children's meals and high chairs and an alcohol licence for the adults.

Ravenscourt Park Tea House

Ravenscourt Park, Paddenswick Road, W6
Tel: 020 8748 1945
Transport: Ravenscourt Park LU
Open: Daily 8.30am-4pm (hot food 11.30am-3pm)

This is a family-friendly haven surrounded by the park's greenery. There's an enclosed garden area with large wooden tables and benches. Otherwise, you can sit inside the cream-coloured café, which has high chairs, newspapers, and a wide range of cakes, snacks and full meals – all freshly made in their kitchen.

Riverside Café

Morden Hall Park, Morden Hall Road, Morden, SM4
Tel: 020 8545 6850
Transport: Morden LU; Morden Road,
South Merton or Morden South Rail
Open: Daily 10am-5pm (closed 25 & 26 Dec and 1 Jan)

Overlooking the River Wandle, the café serves coffee, lunches and teas, and also has a gift shop.

White Lodge Café

Springfield Park, Springfield Lane, Upper Clapton, E4
Tel: 020 8806 0444/020 8442 4284
Transport: Clapton Rail
Open: Daily 7.30am-9pm (summer), daily 7.30am-dusk (winter)

Best enjoyed in the summer when the drawing room café inside this old mansion house opens its huge French windows leading out to the garden. Staff are friendly and the menu features organic juices, all day breakfasts, children's meals and generous salads.

Park Events

Kenwood House Concert

Many of London's parks often confirm their activities pretty close to the day, so it's always best to phone to check whether expected events – particularly non-corporate ones – are taking place. Annual treats come in the form of live music or drama performances in some of the larger spaces like Regent's Park or Holland Park, who have created institutions out of their respective theatre and music shows. Privately organised events like the semi-regular Cannabis Festival at Brockwell Park are very much down to individual organisers, and are therefore not the responsibility of the park itself.

As well as a few of London's annual park events, this section also lists the contact details of the boroughs that are responsible for some of London's major firework displays that take place on or around 5 November in many of the parks listed within this guide. The councils can be contacted for details of prices, best parking spots or notices of cancellations (usually due to bad weather), which should all be taken into account during the pyrotechnics season. You can also go to the Visit London website at *www.visitlondon.com* for details of fireworks displays in London.

May

Afro Hair and Beauty Show

Alexandra Palace Way, N22
Tel: 020 8365 2121

The last Bank Holiday in May sees the Afro Hair and Beauty Show at Alexandra Palace and Park. Still going after almost 30 years, it's a chance to see a fashion show, hairstyling demonstrations and to pick up a few products along the way.

Cannabis Festival

Brockwell Park, SE24
Tel: 020 7926 1000
or Cannabis Coalition 020 7737 3044

Organised by the International Cannabis Coalition, this festival starts with a march that pulls in over 30,000 people and follows a route from Kennington Park to Brockwell Park via Brixton. Floats, banners and a huge sound system make the march a lot of fun and an entertainment licence means live music and comedy shows at Brockwell Park after the rally. Stalls selling food, clothes, and cannabis related wares are all part of the day.

May-September

Regent's Park Open Air Theatre

Inner Circle, Regent's Park, NW1
Tel: 0870 154 4040 (booking line)

The open air theatre has been a permanent feature of Regent's Park since 1932 (see page 22). Every summer between late May and early September the theatre stages shows that in the past have included *A Midsummer Night's Dream, Twelfth Night* and *Wind in the Willows*. They also stage late night shows and Sunday night comedy. The theatre is served by a buffet and BBQ or you can bring your own picnic.

June-July

Clapham Festival
Clapham Common, SW4
This annual festival features indoor and outdoor events including school fêtes, angling competitions, exhibitions, live bands and the Gay Queen of Clapham beauty contest.

June-August

Opera Holland Park
Holland Park, W8
Tel: 0845 230 9769 (booking line)
Website: www.operahollandpark.com
The Holland Park opera season has included amongst its performances Verdi's *Macbeth*, *Madame Butterfly* by Puccini and *Eugene Onegin* by Tchaikovsky. See website for details of what's on.

London Open Garden and Squares Weekend
Website: www.opensquares.org
Open: Mid-June annually
Run by the London Garden and Parks Trust, this is the one weekend when many of London's private garden squares and other gardens open their gates to the public. A number of special activities take place in selected public gardens.

July

Hampton Court Palace Flower Show
East Molesey, Surrey, KT8
Tel: 0870 751 5175/ 0870 752 7777
Transport: Hampton Court Rail or riverboat from Westminster or Richmond to Hampton Court Pier

The world's largest horticultural show with visitors able to browse in a series of show gardens. In addition there are over 150 specialist nurseries from around the UK offering plants galore, gardening accessories and a bumper amount of roses in bloom.

Lambeth Country Show

Brockwell Park, SE24
Tel: 020 7926 1000

Around 100,000 people attend this annual two-day urban show that's regularly held in Brockwell Park. The countryside is the theme and there are stalls selling food, clothes, books and crafts. Live bands are also a major part of the event.

Pride Parade and Rally

Hyde Park to Victoria Embankment

The annual Pride London event usually takes the form of a mid-morning parade in Hyde Park. The huge collection of floats, dancers and bands then travel down Piccadilly and Whitehall, and past the Houses of Parliament, eventually stopping at Victoria Embankment. The day usually ends with an afternoon of speakers, community stalls and music in Trafalgar Square.

Summer Swing at Kew Gardens

Kew, Richmond, TW9
Tel: 020 8332 5000
Transport: Kew Gardens LU & Rail or Kew Bridge Rail/riverboat to Kew Pier

An annual series of open air concerts set against a beautiful botanical backdrop. Anything and everything from jazz, hip hop, classical, world and big band music is played by international artists.

July-Aug

Kenwood House Picnic Concert Series

Kenwood House, Hampstead Heath, NW3
Tel:020 8348 1286/ booking 0870 890 0146

Kenwood's tradition of outdoor concerts has been going for fifty years. It takes place every weekend throughout the summer. Jamie Cullum, The Gypsy Kings, Bryan Ferry and Jools Holland have all performed here and there are also themed nights such as Music to Watch Girls By and Last Night of the Kenwood Proms. Visitors can buy tickets for the area at the front of the stage, or take a picnic and listen to the music from one of the hills around the Kenwood site. Events are subject to change, so it's best to call before setting out.

Kenwood House

August

Carnaval Del Pueblo

Burgess Park, Albany Road, SE5
Tel: 020 7525 5000
Website: www.carnavaldelpueblo.co.uk

This is the largest Latin American festival in the UK, with an audience of around 80,000 people. It starts with a carnival float that travels through Peckham before arriving at Burgess Park. Here there's a main stage with headline artists from Brazil, Mexico and the Andean countries. There's also a huge funfair, a salsa show, salsa competition and dance classes.

Vibrations

Burgess Park, Albany Road, SE5
Tel: 020 7525 5000

A day of celebration of black and Afro-Caribbean culture. Among the attractions are three performance stages, food stalls and children's areas. The Southwark Youth Carnival float travels through South Peckham and finishes inside the park.

November

London to Brighton Veteran Car Run

Starting at Serpentine Road, Hyde Park, W2
Tel: 01280 841 062

The world's longest-running motoring event involves around 400 pristine vintage cars. They leave Hyde Park at around 7.30am and follow a route via Parliament Square, Westminster Bridge and on through the streets of south London to Brighton. The 1953 film *Genevieve* concerns itself with the story of two rivals in this event.

Firework Displays

Alexandra Palace Park, N22 - *Haringey Borough Council* 020 8489 0000
Battersea Park, SW11 - *London Borough of Wandsworth* 020 8871 6000/7534
Bishop's Park, SW6 - *London Borough of Hammersmith and Fulham* 020 8748 3020
Brockwell Park, SE24 - *London Borough of Lambeth* 020 7926 1000/6212
Burgess Park, SE5 - *London Borough of Southwark* 020 7525 5000/0772
Crystal Palace Park, SE20 - *London Borough of Bromley* 020 8464 3333
Finsbury Park, N4 - *London Borough of Haringey* 020 8489 0000
Greenwich Park, SE10 - *Westminster City Council* 020 7641 6000
Hyde Park, W2 - *Westminster City Council* 020 7641 6000
Morden Hall Park, SM4 - *Merton Borough Council* 020 8274 4901
Ravenscourt Park, W6 - *London Borough of Hammersmith and Fulham* 020 8748 3020
Victoria Park, E3 - *Tower Hamlets Borough Council* 020 7364 5000

Usefull Addresses

City of Westminster Archive Centre
10 Ann's Street, SW1P
Tel: 0207 641 510

London Metropolitan Archives
40 Northampton Road, EC1R
Tel: 0207 332 3820

Additional Picture Credits
p.32, p.85 © Vero Pfeiffer / p.37, p.90, p.104, p.107 © Metro / p.135 © Museum of Garden History / p.152, p.156 © Historic Royal Palaces / p.154 © Chelsea Physics Garden / p.165 © Kew Garden / p.176, p.186, p.190 © Kenwood House / p.178 © Royal Borough of Kensington and Chelsea

Bibliography

Bygone Pleasures of London, *W. S Scott* (London 1948)

Exploring London's Gardens, *Lorna Lister* (Lorna Lister 2001)

London Parks and Gardens, *M. Brace and E. Frankel* (Pevensey P 1986)

London's Parks and Gardens, *J. Billington, S. Lousada* (Frances Lincoln Publishers Ltd 2003)

The Royal Parks of London, *Guy Williams* (Academy Chicago Pub 1985)

Walking London's Parks and Gardens, *G. Young* (New Holland 1998)

London and Its People, *John Richardson* (Ebury Press 1995)

Oxford Dictionary of London Place Names, *A. D. Mills* (Oxford University Press 2004)

A Literary Guide to London, *Ed Glinert* (Penguin Books Ltd 2000)

A Taxi Driver's Guide to London, *S Raingold* (Foulsham 1973)

Walking Notorious London, *Andrew Duncan* (New Holland UK 2004)

The Green London Way, *Bob Gilbert* (Lawrence & Wishart Ltd 1991)

Terence Conran on London, *Terence Conran* (Conran Octopus 2004)

Georgian London, *John Summerson* (Yale University Press 2003)

The Lost Rivers of London, *Nicholas Barton* (Historical Publications 1992)

Blue Guide London, *Roger Woodley* (A & C Black 2002)

London's Secret History, *Peter Bushell* (Constable 1983)

The Open Spaces of London, *A. Forshaw & L. Bergstrom* (Allison & Busby 1986)

The Annals of London, *J. Richardson* (Weidenfeld Nicolson Illustrated 2001)

A Walk Round London's Parks, *Hunter Davies* (H Hamilton 1983)

American Walks in London, *R. Tames* (Weidenfeld Nicolson 1996)

Underground London, *Stephen Smith* (Abacus 2005)

London (The Biography), *Peter Ackroyd* (Vintage 2001)

London: A Short History, *A N Wilson* (Phoenix 2005)

The Worldwide Guide to Movie Locations Presents: London, *Tony Reeves* (Titan Books 2003)

The Peopling of London (Fifteen Thousand Years of Settlement from Overseas), *Nick Merriman* (Museum of London 1993)

Index

Order our other Metro Titles

The following titles are also available from Metro Publications. Please send your order along with a cheque made payable to Metro Publications to the address below. Postage and packaging free.

Alternatively call our customer order line on **020 8533 7777** (Visa/Mastercard/Switch), Open Mon-Fri 9am-6pm

Metro Publications
PO Box 6336, London N1 6PY
info@metropublications.com
www.metropublications.com

London Market Guide
Andrew Kershman
£6.99 ISBN 1-902910-14-1

Bargain Hunters' London
Andrew Kershman
£6.99 ISBN 1-902910-15-X

Food Lovers' London
Jenny Linford
£8.99 ISBN 1-902910-22-2